FAR BEYOND THE SHOE BOX

Fifty Years of the National Athletic Trainers' Association

Richard G. Ebel

CUSTOM PUBLISHING

NEW YORK · CHICAGO · WASHINGTON D.C. · LOS ANGELES · TORONTO

Cover Photo: Athletic trainers gathered at the Muehlebach Hotel in Kansas City, Missouri for the first meeting of the National Athletic Trainers' Association.

CIP Data is available.
Printed in Canada
10 9 8 7 6 5 4 3 2 1

ISBN 0–8281–1320–3

TABLE OF CONTENTS

FOREWORD

To the members of the National Athletic Trainers' Association:

The NATA is proud of its forefathers and their legacy chronicled in *Far Beyond the Shoe Box*. This book will record the history of our association and will help the members of today and tomorrow understand, respect and cherish the roots of our profession and association.

As you read and reflect on our history, you will gain a heightened appreciation of the numerous challenges that arose in the beginning. You will learn of the courage and determination shown by those who have helped us not only overcome those challenges but also make significant advances in our first half-century. After reading this book, I believe you will experience an enthusiasm and willingness to accept the responsibility to generate your own professional contribution to the NATA as we enter the next millennium.

This history will describe our first members and take you back to the scene of our first national convention. It will help you appreciate the diversity that has developed as the NATA has become a treasured international institution: from the swelling ranks of people of multiple ethnic backgrounds to the impact of women in our profession to the shift toward globalization, the profession is encompassing more and more as a new century approaches.

The knowledge we glean from our past will assist us in developing and achieving our long-range objectives, so please, make the most of this history as we look toward the future.

—Kent P. Falb, ATC, PT
President, National Athletic Trainers' Association

ACKNOWLEDGMENTS AND CLARIFICATIONS

As an outsider, one who is experienced in the workings of trade and professional associations but heretofore a stranger to athletic training, I can't help but marvel at the remarkable transformation that has changed the face of the profession. All the more impressive is the fact that such astonishing progress is largely the inspired work of volunteers. These volunteers have taken the profession and the NATA "Far Beyond the Shoe Box" to an international organization. This is quite a feat.

Just as these accomplishments must be credited to a legion of athletic trainers and friends of the profession, the writing of this history, too, is the product of many individuals.

My personal gratitude begins with the History & Archives Committee and the 50th Anniversary Task Force. The Committee and Task Force provided the direction for the history, and I have tried to follow it faithfully. I extend a special thanks to Martin Baker, who developed the outline for this book, and to Frank George, who chaired the 50th Anniversary Task Force.

Then there are the NATA members who were interviewed, either personally or in recording sessions in Baltimore and Dallas. Their answers to questions and their impressions as eye witnesses to events were critical to my research. So, sincerest thanks to Marjorie Albohm, Hazel Ando, Ronnie Barnes, Bob Behnke, Ben Carbajal, Janice Daniels,

Gary Delforge, James "Doc" Dodson, Kent Falb, Denise Fandel, Marcia Grant Ford, Paul Grace, Katie Grove, Bobby Gunn.

Also to John Harvey, Peggy Houglum, Ken Knight, Julie Max, Lindsy McLean, Paul Newman, Jack Rockwell, René Revis Shingles, Mark Smaha, Clint Thompson, Karen Toburen, Frank Walters and Keith Webster.

Thanks also to Eve Becker-Doyle and her staff, particularly Teresa Foster Welch. As coordinator of this project and editor of the book, she was my indispensable partner.

Achieving accuracy is perhaps the biggest challenge for any author of a history. And it's easier said than done. Relying on correspondence, published information—often conflicting, and the memories of those who witnessed events, well, it's a process that has its perils. But there is no other way to do it. So, I am certainly appreciative of the "review board"—those anonymous individuals who pored over sections of the manuscript to help ensure that we "got it right."

Some explanations are in order, too. First, readers used to seeing "ATC" as suffixes to certified athletic trainers' names in published works will undoubtedly note their omission on the following pages. With only a few exceptions, everyone mentioned in this history is a certified athletic trainer, "grandfathered" or otherwise. We believe the narrative flows better by dispensing with superfluous material, including the designation.

The NATA Board of Directors in 1997 adopted *certified athletic trainer* as the proper appellation for its members. That term, and the term *athletic trainer*, are used faithfully throughout this book. Exceptions to this consistency appear in quoted material. As an adherent to journalistic orthodoxy, I'm averse to tampering with quotes. It will get you nothing but trouble.

In telling a story—and that is what we are doing in this history—the constraints of space mean that something or someone has been left out.

Consequently, the contributions of many individuals have, of necessity, been omitted. That is a regret experienced, I think, by almost all authors. But since we could not possibly be all-inclusive, we have tried to be at least representative.

In reflecting on the first 50 years of NATA and the profession, the word "glorious," in my opinion, is not too pretentious a term to describe that story. Fortunately, it is a story without an ending. And based on the beginning, my guess is that certified athletic trainers in years to come will find the next installment to be even more exhilarating.

—*Rick Ebel*

1

WAY BACK WHEN

Big Monk, Snapper, Scrap Iron, Kickapoo. With nicknames like these, the early athletic trainers of America could easily be dismissed as idiosyncratic characters inviting belittling assessments from the uninitiated and the ill-informed.

All of which confirms the folly of snap judgments.

True, early athletic training could not, without a wink, be gilded as a profession. The men (and at the time, it was men only) who provided care and conditioning for athletes did so with raw competence unsupported by much formal education or research. Yet, they were tested at every practice and competitive event. And so many of these men responded with an abundance of character, a passion for service and a nobility of selflessness. More important to those who would follow them, they had the columbine vision of explorers.

The cradle of athletic training was most likely ancient Greece, where athletics was revered. The Greeks, as always, had a word for it. Actually, several words, one of which was *paidotribes,* or "boy rubber." The descriptive terms suggested that massage was an important function of trainers. Of the Grecian athletic trainers, the most renowned was Herodicus of Megara, a physician who had the great Hippocrates as a tutor.

After the fall of Rome, athletic training languished. The only interest of nations in body strength and physical contest involved warfare, pillaging and other barbaric pleasures—one reason the period is called the Dark Ages.

The pendular swing back to athletics was a long time coming. Finally, in the 19th Century, interest in gymnastics was revived with a helping hand in Germany from Friedrich Jahn, who introduced the horizontal, parallel and side bars, the balance beam and jumping events. In the United States, Dr. Dudley Allen Sargent taught gymnastics at several universities around the time of Civil War, and two decades later European immigrants imported the sport to the cities in which they settled.

Concurrently, team sports became part of the American scene. In 1869, Rutgers and Princeton, each fielding 25 men, introduced what some looked upon as recreational mayhem, football. By 1905, as a result of 18 deaths and 159 serious injuries that year, President Theodore Roosevelt was threatening to abolish football as an intercollegiate sport.

During this period, the treatment of athletic injuries was handled by the coach or team physician, and the presence of an athletic trainer was a rarity. One notable exception was Harvard University, which in 1881 hired James Robinson as athletic trainer. Another early athletic trainer—and acknowledged by many to be the first—was Michael C. Murphy. He coached and trained track teams at Yale and the University of Pennsylvania until his death in 1913.

Primordial athletic training and its evolution were described in colorful hyperbole by Arthur D. Dickinson, University of Northern Iowa. In a 1956 speech to the American Association of Health, Physical Education and Recreation, he said:

> . . . the word "trainer" has stuck like a bloody tick from the time race horses demanded a valet, who slept in the stables and probably shared part of the horse's menu. Following this, the boxing profession broke out with a rash of handlers— men who appeared at the ring side with a bucket and sponge and hurled meaningless advice to the toiling gladiators, and later slapped the hell out of them when they got them on a rubbing table after the bout. These also were called trainers. Universities and colleges back in the salad days when a forward pass was spoken of in awed whispers figured that if race horses and boxers could stand up under the treatment meted out by these characters, why wouldn't it be a good thing for the football team? So, they lowered themselves socially and hired these chaps who left the ring side and stables in droves. So much chewing tobacco was sprayed on the dressing room walls of our institutions of higher learning that Congress nearly went into an extra session to pass laws preventing such things. . . . Soon college presidents, tiring of

having men on the staff who signed the payroll with an X, demanded at least an 8th grade diploma. At this point, education took a gigantic step forward.

But that was then. "Now," declared Dickinson in 1956, "the modern trainer is as different from the old as the modern surgeons at the Mayo Clinic are from the old Civil War sawbones."

Helping bring about that progress were a number of durable pathfinders. Among them, Oliver J. DeVictor, who started at the University of Missouri in 1913. A year later, Jack Heppinstall entered athletic training at Michigan State University, and Matt Bullock began conditioning University of Illinois teams under the legendary Bob Zuppke. In 1922, Eugene "Scrap Iron" Young was at Notre Dame, and Henry Schmidt began a long run in the Santa Clara University training room in 1926. Some like Claude "Big Monk" Simons, Sr., head athletic trainer at Tulane from 1921–1943, had a dual career. He was also head coach for Green Wave basketball, baseball, track and boxing teams.

Professions and crafts die in infancy unless someone who knows how to execute them is willing to share that knowledge. For athletic training, that someone was Samuel E. Bilik. In 1914, Bilik enrolled in the pre-med program at the University

---

DR. SAMUEL E. BILIK

The man who many would later acclaim as the "Father of Athletic Training" enrolled in the University of Illinois pre-med program in 1914. "Not a cent to my name," he would say. "Bob Zuppke [the legendary football coach] got me a part-time job assisting in training at a dollar an afternoon."

Dr. Bilik was a quick study. By 1916, he had published *Athletic Training,* the forerunner of *The Trainers Bible,* believed by many to have been the first publication devoted exclusively to athletic training.

"About 1926, I started giving intensive summer courses for trainers," he said. "For six to eight hours daily, I pounded away that training, even as medicine,

had to based on sound, logical, physiological, scientific facts and not be a mere slum gullion of empiricism, panaceas, brainstorms of the oddballs."

The firm founded by Dr. Bilik, the Athletic Supply Co. in New York, was said to be the only place at one time where training room products could be obtained.

In January 1949, Dr. Bilik, then on the staff of Bellevue Hospital in New York, brought a small group of athletic trainers together. The upshot of that meeting was the founding of the Eastern Athletic Trainers Association, an organization which soon would comprise Districts 1 and 2 of NATA.

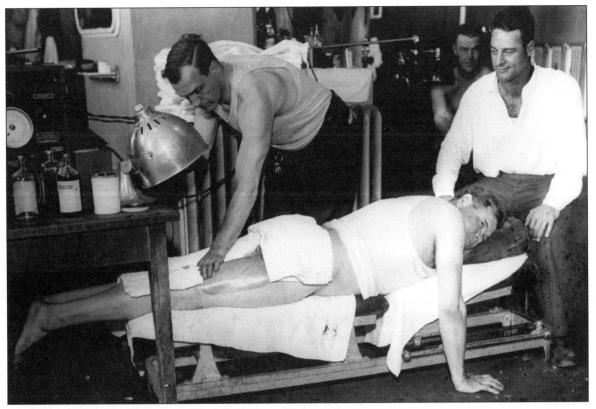

Baseball legends Babe Ruth and Lou Gehrig in the Yankees athletic training room.

of Illinois, where he worked afternoons as an athletic trainer. Two years later he published *Athletic Training,* the forerunner of the profession's authoritative resource, *The Trainers Bible.* For this and subsequent contributions, Bilik was esteemed by many as the "Father of Athletic Training."

Much of the early progress of the profession must be attributed to two brothers from Gardner, Kansas: Charles "Chuck" and Frank Cramer. A pharmacist, Chuck Cramer had a sideline manufacturing liniment which he sold to area athletic teams. In 1920, he founded Cramer Chemical Co. (later called Cramer Products Co.) which would furnish supplies to training rooms throughout the country.

Traveling with the U.S. Olympic team in 1932, Chuck and Frank had an opportunity to observe athletic training techniques. They subsequently shared the ideas and techniques they learned and taught novices the basics in a series of traveling workshops sponsored by the company. For decades to follow, athletic trainers would benefit enormously from the positive impact of the Cramers.

With the dissemination of information and education, large numbers of men were drawn to the profession. At the same time, the subject of sports injuries was beginning to capture the attention of medical doctors, even though it would be a distant day before they would consider athletic trainers as members of the same lodge. Illustrating this newfound interest was publication of *Athletic Injuries* by Dr. Augustus Thorndike in 1938. In an historical paper years later, Brian J. McCue would observe: "For the first time, a long experience with athletes and their medical problems was presented by a member of a major university's school of medicine."

Another significant event occurring in 1938 was the formation of the National Athletic

Trainers Association—not to be confused with the present NATA. Architects of this organization, which was founded at the Drake Relays, were William Frey, University of Iowa athletic trainer, and Chuck Cramer.

President of the first NATA was Mike Chambers, of Louisiana State University, and he was succeeded in 1939 by Jack Heppinstall. The association operated with two geographical units. Ultimately, it would hold two national meetings a year, the Western Division assembling at the Drake Relays, and the Eastern Division at the Penn Relays.

The first NATA had little time to take shape before the U.S. began mobilizing for World War II. Overnight, civilians found themselves in uniform, prompting the popular ditty of the time:

> *You're in the Army now*
> *You're not behind a plow*
> *You're diggin' a ditch*
> *You'll never get rich*
> *You're in the Army now.*

The military, recognizing that ditch digging wasn't the best application of some talents, often assigned athletic trainers to their old familiar responsibilities. In the association's journal, Dr. Wilbur Bohm, NATA president in 1943, wrote of the athletic trainers in the armed forces as well as those remaining on campus:

> We men who are serving in the schools are conditioning the boys for service, just as our colleagues working in direct contact with our future flyers and other servicemen are doing. Many of the boys now in our athletic and physical education programs will soon see service. Our job is an important one.

Preparing men physically for the service was an important responsibility, and as battle casualties mounted, athletic trainers found new demands that would greatly affect their profession in years to come. As Leonard McNeal, University of Richmond, recounted in a 1995 *NATA News* article:

> In World War II, you had crippled and wounded veterans. It was the athletic trainer who did rehab for the soldiers—athletic trainers and maybe a few doctors. After the war, rehab techniques exploded. Before 1945, operating on a knee to repair torn

DR. WILBUR BOHM

An athletic training pioneer, he began collecting autographs in 1924, and among his treasures were signatures of Joe DiMaggio and Ted Williams. The autographs and other Bohm memorabilia, including an old training table and human anatomy maps, are displayed at a family museum in Edwardsville, IL.

Dr. Bohm graduated from Kirksville College of Osteopathy and Surgery and began a 17-year career in athletic training at Washington State University. He later worked with professional baseball and football teams.

In 1932, he was one of five men who formed the first athletic training staff for the U.S. Olympic team. Two of the others were the celebrated Cramer brothers. There would be four more Olympic squads that he would treat.

When athletic trainers made their first attempt to organize a national association, he lent his support, serving during World War II as president of the first National Athletic Trainers Association.

Early athletic trainers learned much from Dr. Bohm, who taught and wrote books about emerging training techniques. Along with his distinguished contemporary, Dr. Samuel E. Bilik, he was among the first group of athletic trainers inducted into the Helms Hall of Fame.

cartilage was a very iffy operation. Now a knee with torn cartilage is treated with an arthoscope. It's easy; it's done all the time.

While the shooting was going on, NATA was growing—but not much. Executive Secretary Bill Frey, now serving in the military at Iowa Pre-Flight, reported at the April 1942 annual meeting a membership of 142 persons in three member classes. He also reported a deficit of $41.19 in the treasury. He noted the problems that finances, or lack of them, could cause an association officer. To pay for an eight-state tour to interview secretaries of state high school associations the previous year, he said, "The Athletic Journal Publishing Co. advanced me $100, the remainder of the trip expenses was paid by the secretary from his own bank account."

This tenuous situation gives a clue as to why, when the nation celebrated V-J Day in 1945, the first NATA was no longer around.

2

NATA Inc.

Breaking in the New Model

When the first NATA went down the tubes in 1944, observers could blame it on the disruptive effect of the war and on regional bickering.

"There were many jealousies between the Pacific Coast and New England trainers, and nobody knew who was doing what," recalled Chuck Cramer's son, John, in a 1984 *Journal* article by Gary Legwold. He went on to say, "My Dad went to an Eastern Association meeting, and they kept asking, 'What's your angle? Why would you help us organize? What's in it for you?'"

Such attitudes were to persist for some time. Paradoxically, they co-existed with compelling reasons for unity and collaboration in the profession. Just as the war had taught the nation that splendid isolation wasn't so splendid anymore, businesses, professions and institutions were learning the same lesson.

This unity was first expressed along regional lines as athletic trainers began to organize in conjunction with their athletic conferences. In the spring of 1947, at the annual conference track meet at Chapel Hill, NC, a group assembled at the urging of A.J. Wyre, University of Maryland, and A.C. "Whitey" Gwynne, West Virginia University. This resulted in the formation of the Southern Conference Athletic Trainers Association. In New York City the following January, the Eastern

Conference Athletic Trainers Association was founded. Before the end of the decade that marked mid-century, the athletic trainers of the Pacific Coast Conference and the Southwest Conference had organized their associations.

The athletic training practice needed a clearinghouse for ideas and a venue to demonstrate new techniques and technology. Meeting these needs was not necessarily dependent on having an association. However, if athletic training was to ultimately develop into a full-fledged profession, this would require widely recognized and respected standards. Who—or what—but a national association of practitioners could establish and enforce such standards?

During the same week the U.S. entered a new war, this time in Korea. Athletic trainers were willing to try again at the next level and establish a lasting national organization.

On June 24–25, 1950, Cramer Chemical Co. sponsored what it called the First National Training Clinic, which was held at the Municipal Auditorium in Kansas City, MO. On Saturday morning, the 125 or so attendees (the figure varies in some accounts) were welcomed by Reeves Peters, commissioner of the old Big Seven Conference. Topics for the clinic ranged from "Charley Horses: Demonstration of Treatment" to "Courtesy to Visiting Teams."

CHARLES AND FRANK CRAMER

Surely early athletic trainers must have contemplated the question: Where would NATA be without the Cramer brothers? In 1950, and for the next five years, the answer would be *nowhere*.

Chuck and Frank were the organizers. They sponsored the clinic in Kansas City which served as the backdrop for formation of the Association. Then they nurtured the Association, underwriting its expenses the first few years. Chuck was the first executive secretary, serving until 1954.

With a degree in pharmacy, Chuck concocted a linament which he sold to athletic trainers. In 1922, he and Frank formed the Cramer Chemical Co. (now Cramer Products) in Gardner, KS, which was and is a supplier of products and services to the profession.

In 1932, the U.S. Olympic team for the first time had a staff of athletic trainers, among them, Chuck and Frank. From this experience and others, the brothers learned athletic training techniques, and they were eager to share them with others. Their company sponsored a series of workshops and clinics, which for many years constituted the "classroom" of the profession.

Many athletic trainers found their jobs, thanks to the Cramers. The brothers kept records of job openings, and directed applicants to them.

When Frank died in 1971, NATA president Bobby Gunn wrote a eulogy that was published in the *Journal*:

> Frank Cramer and his brother Chuck will never be materially repaid for their contribution to our profession of athletic training. Granted, the sales of their products to people in the field of athletics has been their livelihood, but their contributions to the athletic training profession have always exceeded their return.
>
> . . . There are few, if any, athletic trainers that have not been helped by Frank and Chuck. They have aided and promoted trainers in so many ways that time and space will not allow enumeration.

Meanwhile, Chuck and Frank Cramer had called a group together at the Hotel Muehlebach. Before they left town, they were able to boast an important accomplishment—the formation of the new National Athletic Trainers' Association.

L.F. "Tow" Diehm, University of New Mexico, remembered the founders insisting on an organization based on "democratic" and "states rights" principles. In correspondence years later, he explained:

"Democratic" meant that all directors had equal power. There were no officers such as president or vice president, etc. "States rights" meant that each district controls the membership of its own territory. No trainer could join the National Association until he had first joined his district, and had been [accepted] by the membership committee of that district in which he lived. In this manner, each district could screen its own members.

The new NATA was to have four classes of membership, and members would pay $2 in dues. To handle the administration, Chuck Cramer agreed to become secretary, and he would serve with a board of nine members, each representing a self-governing district that embraced the regional associations. The first Board of Directors consisted of:

District 1:
Richard Wargo, University of Connecticut

District 2:
Frank Kavanaugh, Cornell University

District 3:
A.J. "Duke" Wyre, University of Maryland

District 4:
Al Sawdy, Bowling Green State University

District 5:
Joe Glander, University of Oklahoma

District 6:
Frank Medina, University of Texas

District 7:
Fred Peterson, University of Wyoming

District 8:
Henry Schmidt, Santa Clara University

District 9:
Henry "Buck" Andel, Georgia Tech

In 1951, NATA again held its convention in Kansas City. Since there were no officers, Frank Kavanaugh, District 2 director, agreed to preside over the meeting. It was an unsophisticated event, practicality and improvisation in place of formality. Many in later years would fondly recall Joe Blankowitsch collecting registration fees and filing them in his cigar box. The infant organization had made it through its first year, not flush, but at least with $595.14 in the treasury.

The year of NATA's second meeting was a watershed for amateur sports. At the heart of the problem was money and corruption, and its insidious repercussions were to have a long-lasting impact on athletics.

In February of that year, returning by train from a game with Temple University, the City College of New York basketball team was intercepted by the New York district attorney's represen-

tatives. The year before, that team, composed mostly of sophomores, had dazzled the nation by winning both the NCAA and NIT titles. Subsequent investigation of college basketball would reveal that between 1947 and 1950, gamblers had "fixed" 86 games in collusion with players shaving points. Explained one player: "I did it because I wanted to grow up. Sounds funny, doesn't it? I mean I was sick and tired of asking my father for money all the time."

At the 1951 NATA meeting, there was plenty of comment and opinion. Said Eddie Wojecki, of Rice University: "You know, I've made a survey of all the schools that have been caught in the basketball scandal and not one of them had a fulltime trainer who travels with their basketball teams and looks after the kids." He opined that players confide in athletic trainers, who would then have "found out about the fixes and would have nipped them in the bud."

But there was work to do at the 1951 meeting, and the attendees were presented with a proposed constitution and bylaws, which they adopted.

Kansas City was also the scene of the 1952 convention. Reporting on this event in a publication called *The Mentor*, Chuck Cramer was jubilant over the association's prospects:

> The fastest growing organization in the athletic field today is the NATA . . . These men are charged with the responsibility of pioneering a profession . . . and a grand one, too.
> Today . . . our colleges are beginning to give majors in athletic training. True, there are only six colleges doing this today, but the long range program of this group of several hundred trainers will little by little dig into the picture and establish a profession that is indeed essential and will some day be a part of every school in this nation.

At the 1952 meeting, the Board decided to revise the "board of equals" concept. It was time to appoint a leader, and Dean Nesmith, University of Kansas, was chosen to be Board chair for the following year.

The year-old constitution was amended at this meeting to extend membership to athletic trainers in professional baseball, football, basketball and hockey. And the entire membership would now have a symbolic identity: The first NATA emblem was adopted.

NATA changed its venue for the 1953 convention, moving to Miami University in Oxford, OH. Dean Nesmith presided over the meeting, and Thomas "Fitz" Lutz, University of North Carolina, was chosen to succeed him as Board chair.

The 1953 meeting marked the establishment of honorary memberships, and the first to receive this distinction was Dr. Robert G. Brashear, team

physician at the University of Tennessee and a principal player in the formation of NATA. Years later he was to tell a newspaper reporter: "The development of NATA was the greatest single thing that happened in college athletics in my lifetime."

NATA returned to Kansas City for its 1954 convention. It was the last meeting as secretary-treasurer for Chuck Cramer, who resigned for health reasons. His son, John, was chosen to succeed him. The incoming Board chair was Ken Rawlinson, University of Oklahoma.

A brief but productive era came to an end at the 1955 convention at Indiana University in Bloom-

WILLIAM E. "PINKY" NEWELL

As Pinky Newell explained it to a writer of a biographical article, "Everyone . . . tried to talk me out of becoming a trainer. No money, it's not a profession, they'd say. But I felt that through a good education, you could improve the profession. I didn't know then that was called raising standards."

The man who would play such a big part in raising the standards was a 150-pound center on some pretty good Purdue University football teams, the last of which was undefeated in 1943. In his senior year, his advisers urged him to study medicine, but instead of joining a pacific profession of healers, he went to the demolition experts—the U.S. Marine Corps. He fought in the World War II battle of Okinawa, and after discharge from the service, he enrolled in the physical therapy program at Stanford University.

Pinky (so nicknamed because of his ruddy complexion) went back to Purdue in 1949 as head athletic trainer. "When I first came to the Big Ten," he said, "one of my good friends and colleagues would go behind a post to tape an ankle so I wouldn't find out how he did it."

That secrecy was the prevalent mindset of the day, and Newell set out to change it.

He became executive secretary of NATA in 1955, and for the next 13 years he used that position to put the Association on a rock-solid footing. Through his advocacy of education, he helped elevate the profession to where its competence and effectiveness in treating and conditioning athletes could not be denied. Undoubtedly, the day of the telegram—June 22, 1967—was one of his finest. He received notification of what he had worked so long and hard for—that the American Medical Association has recognized NATA as a professional organization worthy of the support of the medical community.

Fortunately for the Association, his resignation as executive secretary in 1968 did not mean the end of his contributions. With his customary intensity, he went on to chair the Professional Advancement Committee in efforts that led to curriculum programs in athletic training and to certification. He also developed the fund that raised seed money for grants and scholarships.

To accomplish what he felt needed to be done, Newell pushed himself hard, and when others needed a nudge, he was capable of that, too. Otho Davis, himself a past executive director, remembered: "Pinky would plant the seed and watch others tend to it. But if it wasn't sprouting as fast as he thought it should, he'd put a little fertilizer to it."

ington. During its infancy, the expenses for NATA had been underwritten by Cramer Chemical Co. This enabled the association to gain the stability necessary to survive. Having achieved that, the membership decided that if athletic training was to attain recognition as a profession, it needed to distance itself from a commercial entity. The Cramers were thanked for their contributions in time, money and encouragement. And then the Board chose someone to fill the position which had been renamed "executive secretary." He was William E. Newell, better known as "Pinky," athletic trainer at Purdue University. In the Association's developing years that would follow, it became obvious to all that the Board could not have made a better choice.

Growth and Adjustments

After five years "in business," NATA was sitting with about $2,000 in the bank and had 279 active members, plus associate and allied members. The list of accomplishments may have appeared at the time to be meager. But a number of committees had been appointed, many of which pursued their assignments diligently and productively.

Pinky Newell's appointment as executive secretary coincided with the end of the gestation period for important projects, and soon the work of the committees began to hatch. This was seen in the establishment of a journal of scholarly research and discourse (1956), adoption of a code of ethics (1957) and alignment with a number of organizations, beginning with the National Collegiate Athletic Association (also in 1957), which was intended to help bring athletic training into the mainstream of sports medicine.

What passed as a headquarters for NATA was now at Lafayette, IN, housed at the Lafayette Mailing Service. For many members at that time, the Association was personified by Harriet Franklin, who served as administrative assistant, initially to Pinky Newell, for 15 years until about the time of her death in 1977.

As executive secretary, Newell's duties included collecting dues, conducting the Association's official correspondence and transacting its business, serving as official spokesperson, keeping records of committees and minutes of the Board, planning the national program and carrying out the Board's mandates. These and other responsibilities would have overwhelmed an ordinary competent and dedicated person, but in Newell the Board had an extraordinary volunteer.

By 1966, the Board responded to the need for more management staffing and created the assistant executive secretary position. A past Board chair, Tom Healion, of Northwestern University, was chosen for that post.

One of the executive secretary's duties was membership development. This was being done, and by 1965, NATA had reached an important milestone—1,000 members.

The income that supported NATA came mainly from three sources—dues (which by 1968 were $6), *Journal* advertising and fees for exhibiting at the Association's annual meetings. The last two sources were not reliable for preparing a budget. By 1968, changes were in order. Newell reported that the most controversial item at the Board's annual meeting that year in Houston was a dues increase. As he explained, the volume of business NATA transacted "in the last three years has not increased threefold but to five times as much as it was in 1965."

The Board responded by raising the dues to $15, effective in 1969, and another $5 in each of the next two years.

The Houston meeting was Newell's last as executive secretary. After 12 years of indispensable service, this much admired professional believed it was time for someone else to take over.

That "someone else" was Jack Rockwell, athletic trainer for the St. Louis Cardinals of the National Football League. Executive secretary was now to be a salaried position, and Rockwell agreed to take it on an interim basis while a search committee screened applicants for a permanent appointment. Possibly Rockwell gained a new understanding of the term "interim," for he was to serve as executive secretary through 1970.

Reorganizing in the '70s

Two major developments necessitated Rockwell's protracted stay. The first involved restructuring the organization. It had become obvious to the Board that if NATA was to sustain and enhance its level of services while absorbing a burgeoning membership, the Association needed a structural overhaul and some definition of responsibilities.

Beginning in 1968, plans for the reorganization were explored first by an ad hoc committee chaired by William H. Chambers, Fullerton Junior College. Later, these were refined by a group chaired by Richard E. Vandervoort, Houston Rockets, who had claimed the distinction of being NATA's first student member.

Completed in 1972, the two-year reorganization was designed to allow the Association to function more effectively and to expand services to

members. To accomplish these goals, a table of organization was established, and this included consolidating committees under four divisions, each headed by a division director.

The reorganization also clarified the responsibilities for administration and governance. The committees would make recommendations, but the Board of Directors, as the legislative body, would decide which to accept for implementation.

The office of Board chair was eliminated in favor of a president. He or she would serve as official spokesperson for the Board and the membership concerning public relations and speaking engagements. The official spokesperson concerning NATA business affairs would be the executive director, who was also charged with implementing the mandates and policies of the Board.

Under procedures of the reorganization plan, members would elect a president, choosing from two candidates submitted by the Board. Presidential terms were to be for two years, and a second term was permitted. For NATA's first president, the members in 1970 chose Lamar University athletic

---

FRANK GEORGE

For Frank George, serving as NATA's president from 1974 to 1978 was an honor. It was also, he said, "the hardest thing I ever had to do with NATA."

Two of the hallmarks of his presidency were the initiation of state licensure and carrying out certification. As in any major change, there was substantial member resistance. He and his Board labored long and hard to win member acceptance.

"As much as we're close and friendly, there weren't many things we all agreed on," he declared. Even on something like a recommendation to prohibit spearing

in football. "Believe it or not, that was controversial even among our own members—they didn't want to be going against the football coaches."

Less demanding but certainly fulfilling for him was his tenure as chair of the Grants and Scholarship Committee. "I enjoyed raising money and distributing it to athletic trainers," he said.

A student athletic trainer at the University of Massachusetts, he enjoyed his work so much he switched his major from business to physical education. After Army service, he embarked upon a career in the training room of Brown University.

In the 1980 Winter Olympics at Lake Placid, George was one of two athletic trainer supervisors. Of working with 30 athletic trainers from around the U.S., he said: "We became good friends. We lived together in the same house—it was like a fraternity house—and we had access to all the Olympic sites. It was the highlight of my career."

ROBERT H. "BOBBY" GUNN

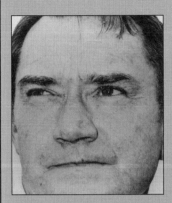

Although he was registered for that very first meeting of NATA, it wasn't until the second one—in 1951—that Bobby Gunn actually attended. "It was an education to sit and listen to those guys talk," he said. "The intent in organizing ourselves was to learn from each other, to have an opportunity to swap knowledge and to get a cohesiveness. This neophyte group didn't have people writing articles and things like that. We had to share our knowledge."

Gunn went on to become NATA Board chair in 1967–68 and return as president in 1970–74. This was a significant period for the Association, because the Reorganization Plan was being initiated and imple-mented. It was also a time for upheaval and innovation in education as certification was being introduced.

With such substantial changes, there would obviously be some disagreements. "When I was chairman and later president, if you had something to say at a Board meeting, you said it. It was just short of war at times. But that's how you get things done," he declared.

After service in the Marine Corps, Gunn studied pre-med at Rice University. But he became an athletic trainer and served at high schools, Lamar University, the Washington Redskins and the Houston Oilers.

He also helped form the Southwest Athletic Trainers Association. "I was the first secretary-treasurer of SWATA because I knew how to type," he explained.

With NATA, Gunn worked with another ex-Marine, Pinky Newell, whom he remembered fondly. He said, "Pinky Newell was a close friend, an ally and an opponent at times. . . . I loved him and he loved me. We could battle like hell and still walk away with our arms around each other."

trainer Robert H. "Bobby" Gunn, a past Board chair. He was re-elected two years later.

Those who pressed for reorganization correctly anticipated the demands on the Association that would be made by a rapidly growing membership in a fast-changing profession. The 1970s would indeed be remembered as a decade of accelerated change, highlighted by the advent of certification to substantiate an athletic trainer's proficiency, the demise of "men only" as a generous infusion of women gravitated to athletic training, and the licensing of athletic trainers by the states in which they practiced.

To properly manage these changes, the Board recognized the need to meet more frequently than just at the June annual meeting. In January 1971, the Board gathered in Houston for its first winter meeting.

At the annual meeting in Houston, the Board had an important item on its agenda—naming a new executive director to replace the retiring Jack

William E. "Pinky" Newell (L) and Bobby Gunn, NATA's first elected president, with Morris Frank (seated) at a 1967 Banquet.

JACK ROCKWELL

A newcomer to the profession, Jack Rockwell was awed by the first NATA meeting in 1950. The pioneers and the people he had heard and read about were there. "I don't think I was ever accepted by them until I was about 10 years older," he laughed.

The early meetings were informal but enlightening, he remembered:

You got ideas, and you got a feeling for things. People did things differently on the East Coast than they did on the West Coast. For the first time, we were able to really communicate with one another, and we didn't always communicate just at the meetings but in those little hotel room things.

Rockwell's first taste of rehab work was up close and personal—in World War II. "I got pretty shot up in Germany," he said.

He was a head athletic trainer with the St. Louis Cardinals football team when he replaced Pinky Newell as NATA's executive secretary in 1968. It was supposed to be an interim assignment while the Board looked for a permanent replacement. But it was a time of transition and new ventures for the Association as reorganization and certification were undertaken. He held the position until 1971.

"We were going through some real major changes. All of a sudden, a lot of people were coming into athletic training with much better educational backgrounds. And we were getting a lot of women into the organization." He added with delight, "One of the first women to be certified took her practical examination in my training room in St. Louis."

Rockwell. The Board's choice was Otho Davis, then athletic trainer at Duke University.

Working on the challenges of the 1970s with presidents Bobby Gunn, Frank George and Bill Chambers, Davis was on his way to becoming an institution. He would one day explain in *NATA News*: "When Frank George asked me how long I was going to be executive director, I remember telling him that I would love to stay until we got the assets up to $50,000." That was to be one of his few miscalculations. By the time Davis stepped down 19 years later, NATA had assets exceeding $3 million.

When NATA members gathered in Kansas City for their annual meeting in 1974, they had occasion to celebrate: The Association's 25th birthday. The events leading up to this milestone were amply recorded in a master's thesis, *The History and Development of the National Athletic Trainers' Association*, by Michael O'Shea, then athletic trainer with the old Baltimore Colts. Six years later the O'Shea

document would be published by the Association as its first comprehensive history.

The 1974 meeting was also notable for a declaration by the Board designed to clarify once and for all just exactly what athletic training was. Approving a Professional Education Committee resolution, the Board defined athletic training as "the art and science of prevention and management of injuries at all levels of athletic activity." The athletic trainer was defined as "one who is a practitioner of athletic training."

In this case, "once and for all" proved to be illusory, for within the profession differing opinions on nomenclature and definitions persisted. Nineteen years after the 1974 declaration, *NATA News* would publish a letter from a venting member: "We are tired of being confused and categorized as the boxer's trainer or the personal trainer who helps individuals with strength and weight loss programs. There is a vast array of names that would better suit our responsibilities to the community."

Revisiting the issue in 1997, the Board proclaimed the name of the profession *athletic training* and its practitioners *certified athletic trainers*. It remains a contentious issue for some, and because there are ramifications, legal and otherwise, beyond what one might suspect of a simple name change, NATA leaders past and present wish it would go away.

Early into its second quarter century, the Association in 1977 relocated its national headquarters to Greenville, NC, where it employed a computer service. This marked the end of Harriet Franklin's long service to the profession. The new administrative assistant was Mary Edgerly.

Poised for Prosperity

If the previous decade was a time for striking and casting, the 1980s could be characterized more as a period of buffing and polishing. Nevertheless, it was hardly a stagnant period. The presidents of that decade—Bill Chambers, Bobby Barton, Jerry Rhea—and their Boards were not given to tepid stewardship. They had important agendas to debate, and many of their decisions impinge upon the Association today.

One decision was to incorporate. In 1983, the letterhead read National Athletic Trainers' Association Inc.

By the end of 1986, NATA Inc. reached a cherished milestone—10,000 members.

Growth in numbers was accompanied by heightened financial well-being. At the 1988 annual business meeting, President Jerry Rhea announced that NATA, which had $2,000 in assets in 1972, now had $2 million. He called the feat "particularly extraordinary in light of the fact that this is basically a volunteer organization."

As NATA concluded its fourth decade, it became obvious that volunteerism alone could not maintain the Association's momentum. Common to virtually all associations and professional societies

OTHO L. DAVIS

When someone from Cramer Chemical Co. relayed a hot job lead for Otho Davis, an athletic director took the liberty of declining it for him. "I told him," he reported to Davis, "that you just came back from the Army and you wanted to finish school, get your degree. And that's what you're going to do."

Davis did get his degree from Lamar University. He spent most of his career with the Philadelphia Eagles. But he was at Duke University when he became executive director of NATA in 1971.

Almost before he had a chance to familiarize himself with the assignment, he took on a major project—securing professional liability insurance for the members. Like doctors, athletic trainers were vulnerable to malpractice suits. "I searched, I guess,

every insurance company in America. No one would insure the members, and we finally hit on Maginnis [& Associates]. . . . They took us and stood by us."

A highlight of Davis's administration was the adoption of corporate sponsorships, the revenue infusions that allowed the Association to accomplish so much more than its limited resources would permit. Two of the early sponsors were Quaker Oats/Gatorade and Johnson & Johnson. Davis explained: "We told college athletic trainers it was up to them to help NATA, not by buying Gatorade, but to have the product on the sidelines for the (television) exposure."

Another goal Davis pressed for was NATA's encouragement of minority athletic trainers. Some of the early meetings had left him in dismay. He said, "I can remember going to the convention in 1957 or 1958, and there was only one black trainer."

Although he hadn't planned on it, he would hold the executive director position for almost 19 years. He was there to usher in a new era for the Association, when it moved its operation from North Carolina to its own headquarters building in Dallas.

1988 Board of Directors: (L to R) Jerry Weber, Denny Miller, Mike Nesbitt, Paul Zeek, Joe Godek, Dennis Sealey, Doug May, Charles Redmond, Terry O'Brien, Janice Daniels (seated) NATA President Mark Smaha and Executive Director Otho Davis.

on reaching maturity is a need to assign responsibilities to a full-time professional staff. For NATA, that also meant finding a home to house that staff.

As president during this momentous transition, Mark Smaha remembered the period as a challenging one:

> We were in the midst of going from adolescence to adulthood during my term of office. It was a significant growing pain. It was like you're a senior in high school and you've grown 10 inches but you're still trying to fit into a pair of pants you wore in the ninth grade. So it was a strenuous time . . . we were not only moving our national headquarters into a large building and becoming much more professional, but moving out of a shoe box mentality into a corporate headquarters in a sense. That was one part of it. The other part was that we were going from a volunteer-run organization from the standpoint of an executive director to a fulltime executive director, and that was a tough, tough thing to go through.

On December 2, 1988, the Association signed on for a new address. The Board purchased the 22,000-square-foot Szor-Diener Fur Co. building in Dallas. Fittingly, when the new headquarters at

2952 Stemmons Freeway was officially opened the following June, it was named in honor of Otho Davis, whose 19-year tenure as executive director was coming to an end.

If there was a pivotal action of the 1980s, the Board's decision to negotiate sponsorships could arguably be described as such. When the Board accepted Quaker Oats/Gatorade's corporate sponsorship in 1985, it was a decision that generated more than mild controversy. But that and subsequent sponsorships also generated revenues that permitted the Association to fund programs far beyond what would otherwise have been possible. It also marked another triumph for the man who championed the idea—Davis.

The Retooling of the '90s

As it entered the last decade of the 20th Century, the first task of the Board was to hire a CEO, and that was done in early 1990. Alan A. Smith, Jr. became NATA's first fulltime executive director.

The second task was to establish priorities and allocate resources so the Association could be positioned for the future. Lawrence-Leiter, a Kansas City consulting firm specializing in associations, was retained, and in 1991 that company began a four-stage program to help NATA develop a strategic plan. The program included a survey of the membership to ascertain their interests, goals and changes they would like to see in athletic training and Association services.

Subsequently, a major overhaul of NATA operational procedures, the first since the reorganization of 1970–72, took place. In 1995, the Board adopted a Governance Task Force proposal to replace the outdated Constitution with new Bylaws. The old Bylaws were revised and renamed the Policies and Procedures Manual.

The changes were more than cosmetic. Under the new Bylaws, key decisions were transferred to the districts. The Task Force noted that business was never really conducted at NATA's annual business meetings, because there were never enough members present for a quorum—better to use those meetings as a venue to report Association finances and information the Board deemed important.

To provide numerical balance among the districts, the new Bylaws also permitted the district organizations to split if they became so large as to represent 20 percent of the Association's membership.

When Dennis A. Miller became president in 1992, he was greeted by Alan Smith's resignation as executive director. Once again a search committee went to work looking for candidates with strong association management credentials. Subsequently, the Board's choice was Eve Becker Doyle, who became executive director in early 1993.

The Bull Market in Membership

NATA's growing financial prosperity in the first 50 years was matched by impressive membership increases. Beginning with 101 duespayers (a figure that varies from account to account) in 1950, the number of members climbed to 773 in 1960, to 1,600 in 1970, to 6,936 in 1980 and to 14,598 in 1990. By the 1999 anniversary year, there were

MARK SMAHA

Mark Smaha started his career with a three-year research project. He and three other beginners—John Schrader, Gary Reinholtz and Rich Carey—conducted the second study ever done on high school athletic injuries. The foursome went on to publish an introductory text for athletic trainers.

Smaha, who spent most of his career at Washington State University as director of athletic medicine, found his years as NATA president, 1988–92, to be a period "of significant growing pains." During that span, the Association would move from North Carolina to its new headquarters in Dallas. It would also transfer the work from volunteers to a full-time executive director and staff.

"Once we got that all settled, we still went through some growing pains trying to get on the right foot with the way we managed the Association," he said. "We went through one long-range plan to determine what our needs were. I thought that was a wise move on the part of our Board of Directors. We brought in a professional group from outside to help us with that."

The two most positive things during his tenure, he said, were achieving American Medical Association recognition of athletic training as an allied health-care profession and the development of the Research and Education Foundation.

Of the AMA endorsement, he said: "It happened during my term. But the person who deserves real credit for that is Bob Behnke [chair of the Professional Education Committee at the time]. He did all the work, he's the one who made it happen."

25,000 members in good standing, and the Association's annual membership retention rate was a remarkable 92 percent!

Despite this growth, it wasn't until 1989 that NATA replaced its photocopied member roster with a printed membership directory. Printing was underwritten by the Quaker Oats Co., and the plan was to publish every three years.

During the first half century, the number of membership classes changed frequently. In 1972, there were 10 classes of members, two of which (Active and Retired) were entitled to vote. By 1991, the classes had been collapsed to four—Certified, Student, Associate and Supplier. Under the new

Bylaws promulgated in 1995, the number of membership classes was enlarged to nine, including four for certified athletic trainers: Regular, Retired, Student and International.

What was responsible for the impressive escalation in membership? Mainly, the heightened popularity of athletics, according to a *NATA News* article in 1991. Interest in athletic training was simply commensurate with greater participation of men and women in athletics. The article did note some other factors: public relations, rising demand for health care, growth in the number of student athletic trainers (attributed to a proliferation of approved-curriculum schools).

3

THE ASSOCIATION AT WORK

The Service Station

In a member satisfaction survey conducted in 1993 by the American Society of Association Executives, NATA members were asked to evaluate their association in five categories. NATA was given high marks by its members.

This was a vote of confidence for the way the Association was managing an extensive array of member services ranging from providing scholarships to conducting education programs to disseminating useful, even vital, information. The organization was clearly in sync with the *raison d'être* of associations and professional societies, which is to accomplish for members collectively what they could not achieve individually.

An early NATA goal was to attract young men—and later women—to the profession. Then help them find work and nourish their careers.

About 1970, a Placement Committee was serving as a clearinghouse for employment opportunities. The Committee operated an information booth at the annual meetings, and it scheduled interviews for employers and applicants. In its first academic year, presumably 1970–71, the Placement Service found jobs for 27 athletic trainers.

By 1982, there were "instant" job opportunities. The Placement Service was offering them on a 24-hour telephone hot line.

Long before the Internet, NATA was attempting to meet members' information needs. The Audio-Visual Aids Committee by 1971 had compiled a bibliography of film, slides, video and audiocassette tapes that could be used for presentations. If an athletic trainer needed, say, something on knee injuries, his bibliography search would lead him to *Different Diagnoses and Treatments of the Knee*, a 16 mm film that could be rented from a Dallas production house.

But the advances in communication technology that took place in the '90s were made to order for NATA. When it installed its web site on the Internet in 1996, the Association's goal was to make information more accessible to members and to answer questions the general public might ask about the Association and athletic training. And for time-perishable data like job referrals, the web site was a natural for those listings.

As member browsers began calling on the NATA web site, they also started taking advantage of the Association's fax-on-demand service. The menu offered instant information on such things as certification and continuing education, meetings and brochures and other publications.

In terms of timely, quality, diverse services, what the headquarters at 2952 Stemmons Freeway was offering members was light years beyond the capabilities of the old mailing service at Lafayette, Indiana.

Scholarships

For many young men and women, a career in athletic training was made possible, or at least facilitated, by scholarships available through NATA. The first of the financial bolsters was the William E. Newell Award in 1971. At the time, the award was $250.

By 1973, NATA also had a Secondary School Scholarship for Student Athletic Trainers "to encourage the continuing education of the individual beyond that of a secondary school diploma"; a College or University Undergraduate Scholarship for outstanding NATA student athletic trainers, and a Post-Graduate Scholarship for Student

---

EVE BECKER-DOYLE

"When I started with NATA," Eve Becker Doyle reminisced on her 1993 appointment as executive director, "it didn't take me long to realize that, by the grace of God, I had fallen into a job that was a perfect match for me."

Her first Board meeting taught her a lesson in member commitment. "At that point, our Board meeting materials filled two of the largest-size notebooks known to man. It became obvious that the Board members read each page of the information with great diligence, and came to the meeting prepared to discuss each issue thoroughly," she said.

By 1993, NATA was still in the trial-and-error stage of moving from a volunteer-managed association to a national headquarters operated by a full-time, paid staff. The transition hadn't been as smooth as Association leaders had envisioned.

Consequently, on her arrival, Becker-Doyle found substantial member distrust of the Board and the national office. She said: "We worked hard to overcome that sense of distrust by improving communication with the members. The Board voted to open its meetings to allow the members to come and observe so they could see how diligently the Board went about its business and how it tried to do the right thing."

Having come from another national association where she served as director of membership services,

it seemed natural that a key priority of her administration—right up there with prudent management of finances and resources—would be member service. But to serve the membership competently, there was a handicap that needed to be dealt with. Neither Becker-Doyle nor her staffers were ATCs; they weren't acquainted with the vexations and challenges that athletic trainers encountered in their work, nor the member needs that required fulfillment.

To fix this, she utilized her visits to members as a crash course in learning about the profession. She brought certified athletic trainers to monthly staff meetings to orient employees at the international office.

Since the first principle of edification is listening, Becker-Doyle sought member feedback. She introduced Idea Cards at the annual meetings so members could submit suggestions.

Not long after she arrived on the athletic training scene, a number of new offerings began to appear in NATA's member-service inventory. These ranged from card programs for purchase discounts to technology-based innovations such as on-line registration for the annual meeting and hotels, fax on demand and web site e-mail. Enhancements were also made in the job placement service.

Of NATA's function, Becker-Doyle liked the analogy of the charter cruise ship. She told members: "The Board assumes the role of the captain, the professional staff acts as your crew, and the members—you—are the passengers. The passengers tell the captain where they want to go, the captain charts the course, and the crew mans the sails."

Athletic Trainers. Each award was worth $500. To get them, applicants needed to pass muster first with the district selection committees and then the NATA Grants & Scholarship Committee, which would pass on its recommendations to the Board for approval.

Financed by private individuals, corporations and scholarship funds, the scholarships proliferated and their value increased. At the end of NATA's first half century, there were 50 scholarships—now offered under the aegis of the Research and Education Foundation, and each was valued at $2,000.

Sponsored Progress

In the mid-1980s, the Board was engaged in debate. There were lots of things that needed to be done, but where would the money to do them come from? Raising the dues significantly was an option, but certainly not a popular, and maybe not even a feasible, one.

The answer, the Board finally agreed, was to tap into corporate self-serving generosity—sponsorships. It was not an answer that resonated well in some quarters. Was the Association exchanging its independence and credibility for corporate gold? Maybe. But on the other hand, hadn't the early Association survived thanks to the largesse of the Cramer Chemical Co.?

In 1985, the Board accepted its first corporate sponsor, Quaker Oats/Gatorade. The money would be used to fund a new public relations program that was being given high priority.

Years later Otho Davis explained that NATA, while taking a leave from the professional sports athletic trainers' success with sponsorships, turned instead to college athletic trainers to help in getting TV exposure for sponsors' products. The college athletic trainers, he said, "wanted something to do, some way to help the profession. Individuals were doing a lot, but we thought we could get college trainers as a whole to help."

Johnson & Johnson soon followed Gatorade as NATA's next corporate sponsor. And in 1989, McNeil Consumer Products joined the team, but its relationship with NATA only lasted a few years.

In 1993, Schering-Plough Healthcare Products Co. signed an agreement to promote with its Tinactin brand a variety of Association programs and activities. Tinactin already was sponsoring what was called a Tough Cases Award. This was to honor athletic trainers who had successfully handled difficult treatment situations.

More recently, the sponsorship ranks were joined by Breathe Right, Sports Guard Laboratories and by that old pillar of the profession—Cramer Products Co.

A dichotomy of revenue generation was now in place. Member dues and fees paid for staff, the legal and accounting fees, the committee budgets. "Corporate funds, on the other hand," explained a 1990 *NATA News* article, "are expected to be used for new research and to support licensure efforts, among other things."

A comprehensive corporate revenue sponsorship program was approved by the Board in 1994, the objective being to increase revenues, visibility and prestige for NATA and the profession. This plan called for the sharing of funds. The district organizations would get 15 percent, provided they agreed not to solicit their own sponsorships from NATA sponsors or their competitors. Another 2 percent of the funds was earmarked for the clinical/industrial/corporate and the college and secondary school practice settings.

Early doubts about the wisdom of NATA accepting corporate money have pretty much evaporated in the face of the accomplishments that money has made possible. Jack Rockwell would later admit: "I fought it for many years. . . . I had some real battles when I was executive director about corporate sponsorship—and I lost. [Now] I think what corporate sponsorship has done for the Association has been tremendous."

The Annual Meeting & Symposia

The big event of the NATA year is the Annual Meeting in June. At this grand convocation, typically 7,500 to 9,500 individuals will gather for workshops, clinics, exhibits and, of course, the annual members' (formerly "business") meeting.

In the early days, these events were pretty much grass roots. The host athletic trainer or district made the arrangements. Housed in a school dormitory, or maybe a nearby YMCA, members paid their $2 registration fee (which doubled as dues) but the bill for most activities was footed by the handful of exhibitors that Warren Ariail had lined up.

"Warren used to handle the exhibits," recalled Jack Rockwell, "and I remember at the end of each convention, my wife would answer the door in our room at the hotel, and here would be Warren with two shoe boxes, one with checks and one with cash. And that's what we operated on from year to year."

The intimacy of the meetings in the beginning years offered a wealth of education, albeit much of it informal. Bobby Gunn, a NATA former president, remembered his first meeting in 1951:

> We all stayed in one old hotel, the Muehlebach. That was nice because as a youngster, I could wander around and get in on those bull sessions, and that was really the learning process at that time. It was great for me. You were welcome to anybody's room where they were having a session. That's how we learned in those days.

In a 1971 *Journal* article, Assistant Executive Secretary Thomas Healion remembered the early meetings:

> There was the favorite meeting of all [1953], the fun in Jay Colville's backyard, and the dormitories at Miami University in Oxford, OH. Not many attended these meetings, possibly 100 or so. But it was always crowded, because everyone seemed to be close.

That setting ended, said Healion, in 1965, when the Association held its meeting in Chicago at the Conrad Hilton Hotel. The days of NATA in college dormitories were over.

Early members may remember fondly the quaint cigar and shoe box files and relaxing at the famed barbecues of the Cramer brothers and Jay Colville; but the meetings could also produce an air of gravity. This was because the meetings were also the drip pans that collected a spate of issues and conflicts. And in the Association's second decade,

---

FRED HOOVER

In 1973, when Fred Hoover became chair of the Convention Committee, registration forms at the annual meeting were still being organized in cigar and shoe boxes. That procedure was still feasible when registrants numbered no more than 300 persons.

It was volunteer labor that got the job done, and Hoover was always quick to credit Tim Kerin and other Convention Committee members and volunteer supporters. "The Convention Committee members and excellent local committees have been the backbone of every meeting," he said. "They do all the leg work, get the speakers, set up the banquets and other functions. I can't say enough about them. . . ."

Nevertheless, Hoover soon realized the increasing size of the meetings would overwhelm the volunteers and result in chaos. By the end of the decade, he and the Committee brought in a firm to replace the shoe boxes with computer registration. Local convention bureau personnel were also hired.

Hoover headed the Committee for nearly 20 years until convention responsibilities were transferred to the international office in Dallas.

In addition to his convention leadership, he also served as Board chair in 1965.

The Cramer Picnic (shown in 1960) was a highlight of the early annual meetings.

there was no shortage of these. In a letter to the *Journal*, Chuck Cramer commented on the 1967 meeting at Columbus, OH:

> Before the meeting there were many notes of discord and discontent. The successful future of the profession was being questioned by many. The arguments and discussions over procedures and methods for professional advancement ran the gamut from reasonable to over-ambitious and from practical to insane.
>
> Somehow, out of a membership of considerate, intelligent and selfless members emerged a spirit that was unwilling to face defeat. Numerous reports following the meeting seem to reflect this same feeling. NATA will survive and grow as a unified group of athletic trainers working together for the profession.

There was definitely no pussyfooting around at those meetings, and Gunn looked back at them with relish. The disagreements served a purpose. He said, "There was a lot of battling going on within ourselves. We were like family. . . . If you had one thought and a few other guys didn't think it was right, then they brought it out. It was very enjoyable in those days. A big fight, but it proved that we could make progress."

The reorganization of the Association in the 1970s produced a number of changes for the annual meetings. The meetings were still the product of volunteer efforts. But there was now a Conventions Committee which would provide better coordination and oversight. Appointed chair of the Committee in 1973 was Fred Hoover, and he would hold that post for almost 20 years.

Of his volunteers' dedication, Hoover declared: "We won an award for having the second-best convention one year in Dearborn, MI, and when they gave it to us, they couldn't understand that we didn't have a professional planner."

By the mid-70s, members from NATA's early days could reminisce about their first annual meetings that differed so much from the ones they were now attending. Association growth was the change agent, which many members viewed with some degree of ambivalence. Dennis Aten, who was serving on the Journal Committee, commented in that publication:

> Growth means more trainers, higher standards, varied programs, greater acceptance and expanded potential. Of course, it also means that we have outgrown our free entertainment at our national convention. No longer will one company be able

to underwrite elaborate get-togethers, trips, meals and other free entertainment which we have come to take for granted. Such is the price of growth.

Increased attendance, however, was giving the annual meetings the critical mass that made attractive new programs practical. An example was the symposium on foot and ankle injuries presented at the 1974 meeting by Schering Corp. in collaboration with the Audio-Visual Committee. Subsequently, the Board decided to co-sponsor these symposia with Schering, and this joint undertaking began the following year with a presentation on musculotendinous injuries.

Enhancement of the product led to new packaging. The convention, the Board decided in 1977, would now be known as the "Annual Meeting & Symposia."

More embellishments of the annual meetings—Free Communications and Poster Presentations—were introduced in 1985. Covering developments in athletic training research, these abstracts were expressed in 15-minute oral presentations or displayed in poster format.

NATA's main event had grown into a something-for-everyone teaching and information bazaar which could only be housed in a major convention center. Karen Toburen, Convention

Tim Kerin (L) and Fred Hoover played key roles in planning NATA's Annual Meetings during the '70s and '80s.

Committee chair in 1999, described the meeting as NATA's "largest venue for offering CEUs, workshops, symposia, mini-courses and advance track." The program at the 47th annual meeting (1996) furnishes an illustration:

- Ten 90-minute labs, where participants practice, hands on, the techniques taught in the lab.
- Thirty-two 90-minute workshops—hands-on interactive demonstrations of current injury evaluation and treatment techniques.
- Johnson & Johnson Sports Medicine Group Symposium: "Respiratory Illness in the Competitive and Recreational Athlete."
- Gatorade Workshop (presented by Gatorade Exercise Physiology Laboratory).
- Two Student Athletic Trainer workshops.
- College/University Student Athletic Trainer Seminar.

Along the way, there was a significant departure in the meetings held by the Board. In 1993, the meetings were opened to the membership. Dennis Miller, president at the time, explained: "We want the members to see what happens at these meetings. I can't think of a better way to learn about your organization than to see your Board of Directors in action."

As the annual assemblies grew from 100 or so registrants to nearly 10,000, the transformation was lamented by many as a loss of intimacy and fraternity. Paul Grace, for many years the executive director of NATA's Board of Certification, saw it differently:

Early on, basically you would come to a meeting, and the registration was being held in a cigar box, and you'd give your $5 and go in. Now, it's via computer registration. The whole sense of professionalism is being developed. At the same time, that spirit of camaraderie, I don't believe is being lost. It shows up in different ways—where in the past you may have had people from certain conferences get together for a social event; now you have alumni gatherings, and you have other events where people still come back together, exchange

L.F. "TOW" DIEHM

Wounded in the World War II invasion of Normandy, Diehm returned to college and subsequently embarked upon an athletic training career that began at Santa Rosa College in California.

For most of NATA's first 50 years, he was a well-known figure in the Association's affairs. He became chair of the Ethics Committee in 1957 and would head that group for the next quarter of a century. He served as NATA's Board chair in 1961.

Much of Diehm's career was spent at the University of New Mexico, where he served as head athletic trainer until being promoted in 1988 to associate athletic director. His memory at that school is honored with the naming of the L.F. "Tow" Diehm Athletic Facility and the Diehm Sports Medicine Endowment.

"war stories" and look to the next meeting. So, it's changed in a sense in size, but I think it's been much more enriched by the diversity that's come upon us.

Compared to the demands of planning and orchestrating a conference the size of NATA's annual meeting, Hercules' housekeeping at the Aegean Stables seems like a breeze. Toburen identified her Committee's No. 1 challenge as running "a quality program based on scientific knowledge. . . . " Next, she said, was providing programs that were diverse enough to meet the needs of members in the various settings.

In order to accomplish these goals, the planners of today's annual meetings look to the members for input. This feedback includes surveys and member ratings of presentations, which are then analyzed. "They [the members] are great at suggesting topics," Toburen remarked.

And of the member complaints and suggestions, what is the one most frequently heard? *Don't run so many sessions concurrently because it makes it difficult for me to choose which one to go to.*

Code of Ethics

An ethical man, Mark Twain once observed, is a Christian holding four aces.

What, then, is an ethical profession?

This was a question early Association leaders ruminated on at length. Given the enormity of an athletic trainer's responsibility for the athlete's welfare, they knew there had to be specific guides of conduct that would be universally accepted by athletic trainers' peers. Without these tenets, recognition by the health-care community would never be realized.

Howard Waite, University of Pittsburgh, and Pinky Newell, agreed to draft a code of ethics. The document they presented to the Board was adopted in 1957. As explained in the preamble:

> The purpose of this code of ethics is to clarify the ethical and approved professional practice as distinguished from those that might prove harmful and detrimental, and to instill into the members of the Association the value and importance of the athletic trainer's role.

Newell would later call the adoption of the code "the most significant action of the 50s." This development, he said, "made the Association responsible. A professional code of ethics is, in a nut shell, a public statement of the expected behavior of any member of the profession."

As the athletic training practice evolved, the code was amended frequently and overhauled occasionally. In 1987, it became one of three components of the Code of Professional Practice. After the Board of Certification (NATABOC) was separated

1998 Hall of Fame inductees Jim Whitesel, John Schrader and Jim Booher (seated, L to R) are joined by members of the Hall of Fame at the 49th Annual Meeting & Clinical Symposia in Baltimore.

from the Association, the Board in 1992 adopted a new Code of Ethics. For the NATABOC there was the Standard of Practices for Athletic Trainers which was devoted to regulating certification.

Activities proscribed by the code include breaches of the Association's proprietary integrity, such as improper use of the NATA logo and fraudulent endorsement of athletic training workshops. The canons of conduct also deal with transgressions that would fundamentally undermine the profession's integrity. An example is a 1974 amendment that endorsed good conditioning and athletic training principles as "the best and safest" program and denounced drug abuse. "Any trainer who violates the stand on unauthorized or non-therapeutic use of drugs for himself or others is guilty of a breach of ethics," the amendment declared.

In 1994, NATA's Code of Ethics got some of the acclaim that Howard Waite and Pinky Newell may have envisioned. The profession's "rule book" was recognized by the American Society of Association Executives with an Award of Excellence.

Hall of Fame

Persons who have contributed significantly to the advancement of athletic training are recognized in nine categories by the Association's Honors & Awards program. Oldest of the honors display window is the Hall of Fame, in which there are inducted candidates selected by the Board from among nominees evaluated by the Hall of Fame Subcommittee.

About the time NATA entered its second decade, a committee chaired by Eddie Wojecki,

Rice University, engaged in discussions with the Helms Athletic Foundation, seeking inclusion of athletic trainers in that group's Hall of Fame. The breakthrough came in 1962, when the Foundation's Board inducted 26 distinguished athletic trainers, all of whom had completed their careers. Among them was Dr. Samuel E. Bilik, acclaimed by many as the "Father of Athletic Training."

In subsequent years, smaller numbers of athletic trainers were inducted into the pantheon that later became identified with various sponsors such as Citizens Savings and the First Interstate Bank.

By 1987, the Association's Board decided to establish a separate corporation "to honor the athletic training profession and enshrine individual members of the athletic training profession." Hence, the inception of the NATA Hall of Fame. Now housed in the Association's Dallas headquarters, the Hall, as of 1998, displayed portraits and biographies of 192 inductees.

4

PROFESSIONAL PREPARATION

The Athletic Trainer as Scholar

Many of the early athletic trainers had trouble with the notion that a career in the field needed to be accessed through a course of study. What was wrong with just a hands-on apprenticeship to a seasoned athletic trainer?

This attitude was captured in one of William E. "Pinky" Newell's recollections:

> They [the old-time trainers] were a little bit jealous of those with an education, and I think most of them were a little bit concerned with their backgrounds. Very few of them had any formal education . . . they learned by doing. A lot of the older trainers didn't want anybody with a formal education. They said they wouldn't work, they wouldn't do the menial tasks like clean the whirl-pools, sweep up, things like that. . . . It was difficult for us to create a profession, so to speak—to raise people up by their bootstraps when they didn't want to help themselves.

But they had to. If athletic training was to win recognition in the health care community, if it was to create opportunities for employment, then there was a need to determine what skills were required to practice and to develop appropriate courses of instruction.

That was evident even before the advent of NATA. The first athletic trainers' association that was formed in the late 1930s planned to teach the necessary skills to high school students. That organization's publication, *The Trainers Journal,* announced the program in a December 1941 article titled, "The High School Trainers Plan in Operation." Lessons appearing in *The Trainers Journal* were to be studied under the direction of team medical supervisors.

Written on the eve of U.S. entry into World War II, the article reported that athletes and student athletic trainers were not the sole focus of the High School Trainers Plan. "There is a defense angle," explained the author. "When the plan gets on in full working force, we can visualize 80,000 student trainers, throughout the country. These boys, a jump ahead of other boys in their communities because of their knowledge of how to care for injuries, may be called upon to help in defense work."

When they met that first time in 1950, the founders of NATA, according to one of them—L.F. "Tow" Diehm—declared the Association's purpose was "to build and strengthen the profession of training by the exchange of ideas, knowledge and methods of the art." The building blocks were to be bonded by education.

Six years after the founding, the Board appointed a committee to research and recommend a program of professional preparation for athletic trainers. Chaired by Pinky Newell, the group, which would evolve into the Professional Education Committee, focused on athletic trainer education and certification.

Three years of committee work resulted in Board approval in 1959 of a model curriculum for athletic training (see accompanying chart). Two important features of the curriculum related to employment of athletic trainers. One recognized secondary schools as employment opportunities for athletic trainers. The course work, therefore, was intended to prepare students not only as athletic trainers but also as high school teachers, primarily in health and physical education.

The other feature was the prevalence of courses in physical therapy, possibly influenced by Newell, who was a physical therapist as well as an athletic trainer.

Newell summed up the effort:

> Three objectives have been satisfied by the program: a curriculum which would give the individual the broadest teaching certificate possible, a curriculum which would have those pre-physical therapy courses acceptable by any AMA-approved physical therapy school, and a curriculum that will prepare men in the management and prevention of athletic injuries.

For William E. "Pinky" Newell, athletic training education was a priority.

1959 Athletic Training Model Curriculum

Physical therapy school prerequisites
(minimum 24 semester hours)
  Biology/zoology (8 semester hours)
  Physics and/or chemistry
    (6 semester hours)
  Social sciences (10 semester hours)
  Electives (*e.g.*, hygiene, speech)

Specific course requirements
(if not included above)
  Anatomy
  Physiology
  Physiology of exercise
  Applied anatomy and kinesiology
  Laboratory physical science
    (6 semester hours,
    chemistry and/or physics)
  Psychology (6 semester hours)
  Coaching techniques (9 semester hours)
  First aid and safety
  Nutrition and foods
  Remedial exercise
  Organization and administration of health
    and physical education
  Personal and community hygiene
  Techniques of athletic training
  Advanced techniques of athletic training
  Laboratory practices
    (6 semester hours or equivalent)

Recommended courses
  General physics
  Pharmacology
  Histology
  Pathology

In a spring 1999 *Journal* article on the history of athletic training education, two leaders in that field, Gary D. Delforge, Arizona School of Health Sciences, and Robert S. Behnke, Indiana State University, called the curriculum important in "identifying a specific body of knowledge for the profession." They also faulted it for relying too heavily on course work that already existed in colleges and universities. They wrote:

With the exception of an advanced athletic training course and laboratory practice in athletic training, the proposed curriculum contained few courses that distinguished it from a typical major in physical education. Essentially, the curriculum represented a "packaging" of the most relevant courses available in related academic areas, rather than an attempt to add new education experiences based on identification of learning outcomes specific to athletic training. This early approach to education of athletic trainers is understandable, however, considering that the athletic training educator had not yet emerged on the academic scene.

The 1959 curriculum model may have been intended as the locomotive to pull the education train, but almost nobody was getting on board. A full decade was to elapse before a college came forth with an undergraduate athletic training program that received NATA approval.

In 1968, a survey of college physical education administrators underscored the lack of progress. In a *Journal* article years later, Gerald W. Bell observed:

The disappointing results of a survey taken in 1968 indicated that half the heads of departments of health, physical education and recreation knew nothing of the athletic trainers' education programs. This knowledge gave NATA the impetus to push for three goals:

1. Develop specific athletic training curricula which would meet the approval of NATA.
2. Carry out certification of NATA membership through a standardized testing procedure that requires a certified trainer to meet minimal competencies.
3. Convince high school administrators and boards of education of the need for qualified teacher-athletic trainers at the secondary school level. Actively recruit high school and college students for the athletic trainer curriculum.

Another *Journal* article, in 1968, indicated there were still miles to go on the road to professionalism. Jack Rockwell cited four typical criteria for determining professional status:

1. Render a unique and essential social service.

2. Establish high standards for selecting members.
3. Provide a rigorous training program to prepare practitioners.
4. Achieve self-regulatory status for both the group and the individual.

"As I'm sure all of you can see, neither our organization nor we as individuals can at the present time fully meet the criteria presented," Rockwell declared. He acknowledged that significant strides had been made, said he hoped through continuing work of committees and allied medical organizations "we can achieve the factors we now lack to become a full-fledged professional organization."

Curricula and Accreditation

As early as 1948, a four-year course leading to an undergraduate degree in athletic training was in place at Indiana University. A year later, the school offered an MS degree in health sciences with a major in athletic training. Indiana's head athletic trainer Spike Dixon suggested this may have been the first comprehensive curriculum in athletic training.

The 1959 Model Curriculum was supposed to have accelerated the adoption of athletic training programs by the colleges. When this did not happen, the Board recognized the need to invigorate the effort.

A year after the disturbing 1968 survey of college deans and department heads, the Board divided what was then called the Professional Advancement Committee into two units. One, the Subcommittee on Curriculum Development, was chaired by Sayers "Bud" Miller, Jr., University of Washington.

This Subcommittee, which would evolve into the Professional Education Committee, was charged with evaluating school programs seeking NATA approval. In 1970, Chairman Miller noted that, of the 42 schools invited to submit their curricula, only four did so. The schools—Indiana State University, Lamar University, Mankato State University and University of New Mexico—were

SAYERS J. "BUD" MILLER, JR.

Head athletic trainer at the University of Washington and curriculum director at Penn State, Miller was a prolific writer, which one might expect from someone with a Ph.D. in English. Few in the profession wrote more articles and books, conducted more research or instructed at more workshops.

In 1969, he was appointed chair of what would become the Professional Education Committee. He directed that group in developing a curriculum evaluation and approval process and in expanding the number of schools that offered an approved program. The Committee also formalized a list of behavioral objectives that represented an early step toward a specialized body of knowledge in athletic training.

Miller espoused the concept of an academic major in athletic training. Unfortunately, this would not materialize until after his untimely death in 1980.

In a *Journal* article, two successors to the Professional Education Committee chair, Gary Delforge and Robert S. Behnke, said of Miller: "His creative thinking and vision provided a powerful stimulus for major changes in athletic training education in the 1980s."

the first to have undergraduate programs approved by NATA.

By 1973, there were 14 schools with NATA-approved undergraduate programs, and only one of them, Indiana State, offered a program for women. Indiana State and the University of Arizona also were offering NATA-approved graduate programs.

NATA approval of programs evolved into systematic campus visitations. Every five years, schools applying to renew approval would be visited by teams under the aegis of the Professional Education Committee. The visitation officers— usually two—would spend two or three days with everyone at the school who was involved with athletic training education. Their findings and recommendations would proceed through channels to the Board for approval.

This procedure was followed until Education Reform, which was implemented in the mid-1990s. At that time, the Joint Review Committee on Athletic Training (JRC-AT) took over the process of programmatic accreditation.

Revised from time to time, the 1959 Model Curriculum continued to govern undergraduate program approval until the mid-70s. By that time, a significantly revised curriculum had evolved, one

that would change the focus from schools of physical therapy to programs considered to be more specific to athletic training. The curriculum revisions were incorporated into *Guidelines for Development and Implementation of NATA Approved Undergraduate Athletic Training Education Programs.*

About the same time, standards and guidelines governing approval of graduate programs were formalized. To complete graduate work, students needed to complete course work in advanced athletic training, laboratory or practical experience in athletic training (300 clock hours) under a NATA-certified athletic trainer's supervision, at least one course in advanced anatomy, advanced physiology, advanced physiology of exercise and advanced kinesiology or applied anatomy.

Delforge and Behnke, in their 1999 article on education history, characterized the mid-70s curriculum model as "limited but identifiable progress toward identification of a specialized, common body of knowledge for certified athletic trainers." Since the revised model contained no new subject areas, they viewed it as "an effort to eliminate irrelevant, or minimally relevant, content rather than an attempt to add new, innovative learning experiences."

The list of schools with approved programs continued to expand. At the same time, the demands of the job seemed to be calling for a broader scope of education than what schools could teach as an academic specialization or concentration. Perhaps, thought some Association leaders, the time had come to ratchet up the academic programs and create and compel a major in athletic training. This notion became a goal that seemed even more attainable in 1979 when Central Michigan University announced a 64-hour athletic training major.

An early advocate of a major in athletic training was Sayers "Bud" Miller, Jr., chair of the Professional Education Committee. Before his death in 1980, he proposed the major as a NATA education goal.

At its June 1980 meeting, the Board said yes to Miller's request. The resolution called for all approved undergraduate programs to offer a major field of study in athletic training by July 1, 1986. That deadline was subsequently extended to July 1, 1990.

The concept of an athletic training major was pursued by John Schrader, Indiana University, who succeeded Miller as chair of the Professional Education Committee. Support for the academic major was buttressed by a Committee survey in 1982–83 indicating that nearly all 62 of the deans and department heads surveyed were receptive to such a program at their schools. With that endorsement, the Committee under Schrader and his successor, Delforge, set out to develop strategic plans for approving undergraduate programs as academic majors.

To determine what an athletic training major should entail, the Association retained Professional Examination Service of New York in 1982 to conduct a nationwide Role Delineation Study. This research, the Board believed, would identify an athletic trainer's responsibilities and the knowledge and skill requirements needed to fulfill them. Everything an entry-level athletic trainer could expect to do—the "performance domains"—and

GARY D. DELFORGE

As chair of the Professional Education Committee from 1982–87, Gary Delforge's biggest challenge, he said, was "trying to create an awareness among college and university administrators as to what athletic training actually is and to get them to accept that athletic training education was arriving as a legitimate area of professional endeavor."

It was a challenge he managed successfully.

The signature accomplishment of the Committee during his tenure was development of an athletic training major, the concept for which he is quick to credit his predecessor, Sayers "Bud" Miller, Jr. The first step was to survey the deans and department heads of the 64 NATA-approved schools to see if they would buy into the idea.

For school curriculum directors, he said an athletic training major "would represent a lot of added courses, expansion of the curriculum, and we were very, very surprised with the positive support."

While serving on the faculty of the University of Arizona, Delforge started the graduate athletic training program at that school. "It was one of the first two graduate programs approved by NATA," he said.

For Delforge, the difference between athletic training education and mentoring is a matter of reach. "Athletic training education," he said, "is imparting the knowledge and skills and wisdom to others who hopefully will accept some of those teachings, sort of becoming disciples. It can certainly affect many more athletic trainers in a positive way than the mentor personally or singly could do."

ROBERT S. BEHNKE

As a member of the Professional Education Committee, of which he became chair in 1987, Bob Behnke saw a lot of history being made in athletic training education. He cited a hat trick of Committee-initiated accomplishments in which he was involved: American Medical Association recognition of athletic training and subsequent accreditation through the Commission on Accreditation of Allied Health Education Programs, development of an athletic training major for undergraduate programs and elevation of graduate programs to where they were truly graduate education.

His toughest challenge as Committee chair was in obtaining AMA recognition of athletic training as an allied health profession and the subsequent outside accreditation. Like any new chair of a committee, he inherited a lot of files. He said:

> After about a year of familiarizing myself with the materials, I noticed that way back in the mid-70s, Bud Miller, who was then chair of the

Professional Education Committee, had sought a similar attempt to accredit the program outside. We were just doing it in-house, so to speak. At the time—it was a very early stage of our education program—the sentiment of the Board was essentially that we were not ready to give up the amount of control that was necessary to have an outside body do the accrediting. And so it was put on file. . . . In going through the files on the concept of programmatic accreditation, I brought it back to the Board and they said, Well, go find out.

Behnke did—and spent the next two years assembling all the materials that comprised NATA's application to the AMA.

The next goal for Behnke and the Committee was to give credibility to graduate programs in athletic training education. Heretofore, it had been possible to use graduate programs as an entry-level route to certification. Subsequently adopted by the Board, the Committee's proposal, said Behnke, "was a true step toward saying 'If you're going into one of our accredited graduate programs, you will already have the entry-level skills and knowledge and you're going to move above and beyond that level.'"

Behnke, who spent much of his career in teaching and in treating athletes at Indiana State University, retired in 1997.

would need to know would be spelled out in black and white.

Based on findings of the Role Delineation Study, the Professional Education Committee developed and published *Competencies in Athletic Training*. Designed to promote true competency-based education, the document was included in the 1983 *Guidelines*.

Components of the athletic training major included the concept of an *equivalent* academic major. This called for athletic training programs to be at least equivalent to the minimum number of semester hours required for any major offered by

the department. The programs also had to meet NATA-specified behavioral objectives.

By the middle of 1990, the deadline for colleges to convert their approved bachelors degree programs to academic majors or the equivalent, all 73 schools had done so.

Buttressed with these degrees, where were graduates going with them? The 1997 Annual Placement Study, conducted by the Professional Education Committee and JRC-AT, found that 36 percent had taken employment as athletic trainers and most of the rest were doing post-graduate work. Placement findings from the 14 NATA-approved graduate schools showed 85 percent went into athletic training. The largest proportion—43 percent—found employment in a clinical setting.

Certification

Important as it was, teaching curricula bearing the NATA stamp of approval was only one hand-hold in the athletic trainer's climb to occupational meritocracy. The other grip would require respected credentials, validated through testing. With that in mind, the Board in 1962 instructed the Professional Advancement Committee to look into and prepare a plan for professional certification.

Nobody expected overnight delivery, nor did they get it. But by 1969, work had progressed to the point where Association leaders began preparing the membership for a seismic event that would transform athletic training from a trade to a profession.

As indicated earlier, that year the Professional Advancement Committee was split into two subcommittees—one for Curricular Development and the other for Certification. J. Lindsy McLean, Jr., University of Michigan athletic trainer, was appointed chair of the Subcommittee on Certification.

"Does the National Athletic Trainers' Association Need a Certification Examination?" This question was the title of *Journal* article penned by McLean in the spring of 1969. The best qualified athletic trainers were leaving the field because of financial reasons and unfavorable working conditions, he wrote, and young athletic trainers were being denied opportunities because their qualifications weren't recognized. He declared:

> The continued existence of such situations obviously does not reflect a truly mature profession in need of no further advancement or reexamination. Realistically, athletic training still has a long way to go if it is to become the

---

LINDSY MCLEAN

Before the game that Lindsy McLean's San Jose State team was to play, the athletic trainer from the opposing team came over to bum some tape. The man's only credential as an athletic trainer was being a friend of the athletic director, who had hired him after the coach pressured a very competent athletic trainer to resign.

"Well," said McLean, "I was a guy who had high aspirations for our profession, and here's someone who has no credentials and can't remember something as rudimentary as tape."

The incident turned out to be the best thing that could happen to athletic training education.

McLean wrote a letter to the *Journal* advocating a certification exam. "We had to establish certain standards before a person was hired," he declared.

Pinky Newell read the letter and asked McLean to head a new subcommittee to develop a certification exam. McLean recalled: "I told him I didn't know the first thing about this. Pinky said, 'It's something that you believe in—you'll find a way.'"

McLean took the assignment in 1968, and the first exam was given in 1971. The subcommittee became the Board of Certification, and McLean headed it while he was athletic trainer at the University of Michigan. By the time he stepped down in 1978, the position had mushroomed to nearly full-time proportions.

Although his accomplishments with certification were certainly not humble, he looked at his handiwork with humility. "I've been extremely fortunate to have been hand-picked to do things that I think a lot of people could have done as well or better," he said.

PAUL D. GRACE

Grace was coordinator of sports medicine at Massachusetts Institute of Technology when he was appointed chair of the NATABOC in 1980. In 1989, he left MIT to become the Board of Certification's first full-time executive director. It was a year marked by substantial change in certification, and some of it didn't sit well with some athletic trainers.

"There was quite a lot of fear that what we were doing would cause individuals not to seek certification, there would be a drop-off in the number of athletic trainers that were entering the marketplace. Just the opposite happened," he said.

Grace retired as executive director in 1997. About his experience, he said:

I'm most proud of the recognition that we've been able to maintain for the ATC credential. The ATC is a statement that we make to the world that, "This individual has met certain standards and we recognize that individual for attaining those standards." And to be part of the team that helped develop and implement how those standards are applied is very rewarding.

profession most of us hope it will. . . . In recent years, there has been much discussion of a possible certification examination for NATA. Many feel that such a practical and written evaluation is the best answer for the immediate problems of professional preparation within the Association when all alternatives are considered. . . . Such an examination would give our Association a unity of purpose and direction at a time when it is sorely needed. Let us proceed now!"

One of the things that McLean and others feared was that unless the profession had a standard of competence, such as what certification could provide, it would be heavily populated by unqualified individuals, namely cronies of the coaches, who would hire them because they could pull their strings. He had witnessed that first-hand, and the experience rankled.

Certification was an easy sell. "The Board was ready for it," said McLean. "Everyone was just as frustrated as I was. We were starting to educate our people, and we didn't have any leverage or any control over who was called an athletic trainer when universities or head football coaches were hiring people."

On something so earth-shaking as certification, McLean and the Board wanted input from the membership. Since many of the members were seasoned athletic trainers whose skills came more from experience than book learning, it was obvious that there would be opposition in some circles to taking the exam.

No problem. That issue was defused by surveying the members. They were told that current members would be "grandfathered"—they would not have to take the exam. They were also asked what topics they thought the exam should cover.

"We got great cooperation from the entire membership. I don't think I got one questionnaire back that was violently negative," McLean recalled.

The Board authorized the American Public Health Association's Professional Examination Service to develop and administer a certification examination. The plan was for 150 multiple-choice questions on such topics as anatomy, physiology, prevention of injury, first aid, recognition of injury and treatment techniques. There would also be oral and practical sections.

McLean remembered the question-selection process:

When we started, we didn't have any money to develop all of our questions ourselves. We went to the Professional Examination Service in New York and borrowed questions from the allied health professions. Back in '69, it was maybe a couple hundred dollars to develop a question from scratch for our own specific field. . . . We would borrow a lot of questions for the first few years that weren't quite applicable to athletic training as we would have liked them to have been. But they did test your knowledge of anatomy and physiology, and people would walk out of the exam scratching their heads and saying, "Boy, that was tougher than I thought it would be." I think that was the goal we were looking for.

Given the diversity of candidates' educational experiences, there was a need for flexibility in certification. Three tracks for eligibility were established. Applicants could be graduates of a NATA-approved athletic training program that included two years of supervised clinical education. Or they could be graduates of a physical therapy curriculum, with a minor in health or physical education, a valid teaching certificate and two years of NATA-supervised clinical education. The third

option was on-the-job training (at least 1,800 hours) supervised by certified athletic trainers, plus a bachelors degree.

Qualifying athletic trainers earned and proudly displayed a new set of initials—ATC, for certified athletic trainer, beginning in 1971. That year, the first certification examination was administered at the District 6-Southwest Athletic Trainers Association meeting in Waco, TX. Twenty-eight athletic trainers took the exam. The number of candidates increased in small increments the next two years. Then, in 1974, the breakthrough—187 candidates.

The passing rate for the early years was 91 percent. For those who flunked, there was commiseration from Sally W. Westphalen, of Professional Examination Service, and McLean. In a 1978 *Journal* article, they wrote: "Those individuals should not be embarrassed by this failure, since certification is recognition only of the highest level of competence in this field."

The rigors of the examination were recalled by Jack Rockwell years later. He said, "I think when some of us who were grandfathered in saw the test, we were actually glad that we had been grandfathered in."

DENISE FANDEL

As head athletic trainer at the University of Nebraska-Omaha, Fandel served as president of the NATA's Board of Certification from 1992–96. After Paul Grace ended his long service as the NATABOC's executive director, that position was renamed administrator of credentialing programs and placed in charge of a full-time staff. In 1997, Fandel was the first to assume that post.

The two main goals she pursued were maintaining the integrity of the ATC credential and making the public aware of how it benefits from those who have earned that designation.

For Fandel, there was no point in just preaching to the choir. The athletic directors and coaches are certainly familiar with what the athletic trainer brings to the table. But recognition by the citizenry that doesn't come into contact with athletic trainers is important, too. The school board members, insurance companies and parents of students not participating in sports may not appreciate how athletic trainers benefit all students, and that's unfortunate, she said.

"Because the athletic trainers are there every day," she declared, "interfacing with students whether they're injured or not, and teaching. So we probably can do more in communicating what an athletic trainer provides to the people other than the ones we come into daily contact with."

As part of the Reorganization Plan for the Association, the Board in 1970 established the Board of Certification (NATABOC) and appointed McLean chair. He would hold that position until 1979. He would be succeeded for a short period by Rod Moore, Valparaiso University, and then by Paul Grace, Massachusetts Institute of Technology.

Grace would head the certification body for 18 years, later with the title of executive director. Under his gifted stewardship, the NATABOC and certification would be transformed many times to meet the demands thrust upon the profession and the opportunities that presented themselves. The certification board would eventually write the examination questions, provide for examiners, conduct role delineation studies every five years and monitor the accumulation of continuing education units (CEUs).

The defining moment of the period occurred when the NATABOC won recognition by the National Commission of Health Certifying Agencies as the official certifying body for the athletic training profession. To comply with Commission requirements, the Board in 1982 granted the NATABOC administrative independence on policy and procedure matters. In 1990, the certifying body was completely separated from the Association and incorporated. Athletic trainers serving on the NATABOC were to be elected from the districts.

In 1997, the NATABOC was restructured. Its president, Brad Sherman, explained, "The Board has become increasingly frustrated because we were getting caught up in micro-management. We were spread too thin in our effort to do all things."

Consequently, the certification board was shrunk from 13 to 8 members, five of whom would be certified athletic trainers and the other three would come from medicine, corporate education and the public sector. Instead of being elected as they had been, the board members would be chosen by a nominating committee.

For Paul Grace, 1997 marked the end of a long and productive career as the NATABOC's executive director. That office became a full-time position:

administrator of credentialing programs. Denise Fandel, head athletic trainer at the University of Nebraska-Omaha and a past NATABOC president, was chosen to fill it.

In its early years, the NATABOC was testing 300 candidates annually. By 1997, that number had risen to 4,500 each year, and the ATC credential was recognized in 33 states as the standard for regulation; *i.e.*, licensure, certification, registration.

Continuing Education

When you're through learning, you're through. This credo of coach Lou Holtz reflected the Board and education leaders' view of certification as being an important education port of call but not the ultimate destination.

"The danger of obsolescence," wrote Sayers "Bud" Miller, Jr. in a *Journal* article, "is probably the primary motivator for athletic trainers' participation in continuing education activities. In fact, obsolescence, with its influence on the care of the athlete, makes continuing education a matter of necessity rather than choice."

He was explaining the Board's decision in 1974 to implement continuing education as a requirement for maintaining certification. To keep their ATC designations, certified athletic trainers would have to acquire nine continuing education units (CEUs) every three years. This could be done by attending scientific workshops, participating in programs at district and NATA meetings, publishing original works, taking correspondence courses in athletic training or related fields.

The CEU idea wasn't everyone's cup of tea. President Frank George recalled the resistance. "Almost no one likes change. There was a lot of footdragging on it. We wanted to initiate it sooner than we did. When it first came in, it was very non-demanding. Meaning you got a lot of CEUs for things you don't get CEUs for now," he said.

George himself was a little unsure. He confessed:

> I'll be honest. I wasn't gung-ho for it at once, because I didn't see how we could possibly keep track of the members' CEUs. You'll have to

remember, computers were just getting going then . . . So, we'd have to bum computer time from our universities to get that CEU thing going. On the first go of it, it was kind of a flop. As in anything, we had to learn.

The proposed 1976 start-up for accumulating CEUs was postponed. George attributed the delay to administrative problems. By the time the first CEUs were recorded—on computer at the 1978 annual meeting in Las Vegas—the number of required CEUs had been reduced to six.

In its 1982 spring issue, the *Journal* began publishing 10-question quizzes that offered .3 CEU credit. Coordinated with a *Journal* article on the subject, the quizzes could be completed and sent, with $12, to the Hahnemann Medical College in Philadelphia for grading. Topic of the first quiz was "The Burnout Syndrome Among Athletic Trainers."

The NATABOC, which administered continuing education, raised the recertification requirements to eight CEUs in 1993. At that time,

it reiterated the avenues for accumulating them, which by then also included certification in first aid, CPR, EMT and participation in U.S. Olympic Committee programs.

Research: The Missing Ingredient Turns Up

To carry the freight of professional acceptance, NATA had spent much of its first half century putting together, through curricula development and certification, a fine railroad. The only thing missing was the tracks. The rails and cross-ties— scientific inquiry that led to knowledge—were not yet in place.

There had been a Research & Injury Committee, the mission of which was to "conduct, document and report research in the athletic training profession." The Committee offered an award to encourage outstanding research.

There was also the *Journal,* published since 1956 as an organ of scholarly discourse, which included research.

MARJORIE J. ALBOHM

Marjorie Albohm's career has been one of firsts or at least being one of the early settlers. She was one of the first—sixth actually—to take the certification exam. Few women before her had served on an NATA committee. And she was the first woman to serve on the NATABOC.

Her vita catalogs a long list of published articles, books and monographs, not to mention instructor assignments at athletic training workshops. When NATA was looking for leaders to fill key positions, she was a logical choice. In the late 1990s, she became president of the Research and Education Foundation.

Of the Foundation, she said:

We're making progress. The challenges are still out there, but I truly believe that our members are seeing the value of the Foundation. And I believe that once that happens, then people outside our group will recognize athletic trainers and will identify us and say, "That is the health-care provider for our future."

While Albohm headed the Foundation, she was also chair of another key body, the Reimbursement Advisory Group, which was seeking to gain acceptance of athletic trainers by third-party payers of medical claims.

She entered the profession in 1972 as an assistant athletic trainer at Indiana State University and would ultimately transfer to the clinical setting at The Center for Hip & Knee Surgery, Mooresville, IN.

"When I started," she acknowledged, "I don't think that I ever thought that I would be given this much opportunity, be presented with this many challenges and have been given so much support by my professional colleagues throughout my career."

But the Association's education escalator was ascending to the graduate level, and that involved programs that were distinguished by research requirements.

Published in the fall 1988 *Journal* was an article titled "Research in Athletic Training: the Missing Ingredient." The author, Louis R. Osternig, University of Oregon, declared:

> Much of what is practiced in athletic training and what is taught about athletic training does not have a base of scientific scrutiny. There is a need to determine those factors impeding progress in this area. Ongoing research is essential if the field is to be credible within the paramedical disciplines and must play a far greater role if athletic training is to continue to be recognized as a true allied health profession.

A lot of heads nodded in agreement.

In 1991, the NATA Research and Education Foundation was inaugurated to expand on the work of the Research & Injury Committee. It was initiated by NATA Executive Director Alan Smith; Jack Weakley, of Johnson & Johnson; NATA Research Chair John Powell, and NATA Profes-

Malissa Martin, chair of the Foundation's Education Committee, speaks at the 1997 Educators' Conference.

sional Education Committee Chair Robert S. Behnke. Governed by a 21-member board of directors, it is a tax-exempt charitable organization separate from NATA.

The Foundation has several committees, including Research, Education and Scholarships.

The Research Committee promotes scientific investigation among athletic trainers, evaluates proposals and makes recommendations for funding grants.

The Education Committee developed and presented educational opportunities for athletic trainers, including home study courses, district lecture series, annual symposia and the Athletic Training Educators' Conference. The responsibility for education program development was transferred to the NATA Education Council's Continuing Education Committee beginning in 1999. Responsibility for raising funds to support the programs remains with the Foundation.

In fulfilling its duties, the Scholarship Committee by 1999 was presenting 54 awards, each valued at $2,000.

Much of the funding that makes this all possible—75 percent of it—comes from nonmembers and the corporate community. The first annual fund, launched in 1995, had an 18-month goal of $180,000. That goal was achieved. Encouraged by this success, the Foundation was undertaking a more ambitious challenge as NATA approached its golden anniversary. The goal was to raise a half-million dollars.

Such challenges, typical of those encountered by the charitable organizations that rely on donor support, were cushioned by the widely held conviction in the Foundation's merit.

"There weren't any obstacles," remarked Ronnie Barnes, New York Giants athletic trainer, in describing his tenure as the Foundation's second president. "We had a blank check. Just go and make a foundation, set up the rules, set up the guidelines, develop the goals and look at strategies. And raise some money."

Marjorie Albohm, who was elected Foundation president in 1996, saw the organization as an

RONNIE P. BARNES

"If you blink, something will change in this Association and in the profession," Ronnie Barnes observed. Since the day he entered athletic training in 1967, he said, "I'm impressed that some part of this Association has moved every day of its existence."

One of the moves of the early 1990s was the establishment of the Research and Education Foundation. Barnes, who had served on the Board of Certification for many years, was named president of the Foundation in 1994.

His primary goal was to raise money and make funds available for scholarships, research and education.

"I think if we can leave a legacy as older and experienced athletic trainers, it would be to enhance the educational opportunities that our students have," he declared. "I think it would be to make them much better than we were, much brighter, much more advanced. . . . So, the Research and Education Foundation is a passion of mine."

That athletic trainers focus so much on education should not come as a surprise, according to Barnes. They are different from those employed in some health-care fields. He noted, " . . . nurses just take care of patients, and physical therapists just take care of patients. Athletic trainers work in a more extensive health-care environment, and often are trained as teachers, so education is very important to them."

historic landmark signifying a level of maturity for NATA. She stated:

> . . . in some ways I think we're a very immature profession, in adolescence as we look to where we will be in future health care. And yet, the establishment of a foundation says this Association and the mission of this Foundation will be here now and for all of time. We establish the certified athletic trainer as a scientific entity through research and education.

Education Reform

At the urging of Sayers "Bud" Miller, Jr., NATA in the late 1970s began looking for an outside agency to accredit its athletic training education programs. Although still viewing that goal as worthy, the Board subsequently found these efforts to be premature and suspended them.

The attempt was revived in 1987 by Robert S. Behnke, who had succeeded Gary Delforge that year as chair of the Professional Education Committee. Two years later the Board adopted the Committee's recommendation to seek accredi-

tation by the American Medical Association's Committee on Allied Health Education Accreditation (CAHEA). This organization was recognized by the U.S. Department of Education as an accreditating agency for the allied health professions. Behnke supervised the extensive process of collecting supporting documents and preparing the application.

For everyone engaged in athletic training, June 22, 1990 was a day for rejoicing. On that day, the AMA House of Delegates voted to recognize athletic training as an allied health profession, thus paving the way for CAHEA accreditation.

This accomplishment was followed by establishment of the Joint Review Committee for Educational Programs in Athletic Training (JRC-AT) by co-sponsors NATA, AMA and three professional societies representing family physicians, pediatricians and orthopedic surgeons in sports medicine. The JRC-AT was then incorporated independent of NATA. Its first task was to develop standards and guidelines governing JRC-AT review and CAHEA accreditation of entry-level education programs.

CAHEA was disbanded in 1994 by AMA, and taking its place was an independent agency, the Commission on Accreditation of Allied Health Education Programs (CAAHEP).

As these events were unfolding, the Board and education leaders were recognizing that the entire education program needed review. The passage of time had left in its wake redundancies and obsolescent programs. These programs could not adequately equip athletic trainers to stay afloat amid intensifying competition in the health-care sea. Nor could they prepare athletic trainers for all of the new work environments that had emerged. Furthermore, the existing system created uneven levels of preparedness for entry-level athletic trainers.

Consequently, a new proposition was placed on the table. Often referred to as "Education Reform," the proposal called for better preparing athletic trainers to meet the demands of the future, to align themselves with other health-care professionals and their credentialing routes, and to improve the public perception of athletic training.

To create the story boards for this epic production, the Board in 1994 formed the Education Task Force and appointed John Schrader, Indiana University, and Richard Ray, Hope College, co-chairs. The Board declared there should be "no limitations on this task force's scope of evaluations and/or recommendations."

With its "no limitations" freedom, the Task Force examined every imaginable aspect of athletic training education. Two years in the making, its report containing 18 far-reaching recommendations was submitted to the Board in December 1996. The Board adopted every recommendation.

One provision of the Education Reform package combined what had become two routes to certification into a single curriculum-based path. Heretofore, candidates had the option of taking programs emphasizing either curriculum or internship. But records of certification exams were showing that curriculum students were outscoring internship candidates in all areas. Consequently, beginning in 2004, candidates would need a bachelors degree and completion of a CAAHEP-

accredited entry-level athletic training program to sit for the exam.

On the other hand, another recommendation called for developing an entry-level post-graduate program that would provide an alternative route to certification. This would benefit students whose situations as undergraduates were not compatible with athletic training education.

To eliminate the duplication of education activities, the Task Force had recommended creation of an Education Council, which would act as a clearinghouse for education policy. The Council would maintain dialogue with JRC-AT on accrediting entry-level programs. It would also accredit post-graduate education programs and act as a resource for developing doctoral programs. Accordingly, the Board installed the Education Council in 1996 and appointed Chad Starkey, Northeastern University, chair. With the formation of the Education Council, the Professional Education Committee was disbanded in June 1998 after 28 years of overseeing athletic training education.

Another important component of the recommendations called for developing multi-disciplinary education programs. These would coordinate athletic training with teaching, nursing, occupational therapy, physical therapy and other allied fields. The rationale here was the belief that, because of economic and other reasons, the future in health care belonged to professionals who were multi-skilled. In a 1998 *Journal* article, Starkey, the new Education Council chair, explained:

> Athletic training education involves the incorporation of no fewer than five areas that could be considered the provinces of other professions. No other profession's clinicians are responsible for preventing injury and illness, for evaluation/ management, for rehabilitation, for counseling, and for education of its clientele. We are the original multiskilled health-care providers, although none of this knowledge or skill is unique to our profession.
>
> Our marketability stems from our ability to combine these knowledge bases, apply them to a specialized population, and capitulate the costs associated with injury . . .

And what might be the impact of the single track route to certification on students considering an athletic training career? In a 1995 *NATA News* article, Paul Newman, chair of the College & University Student Athletic Trainers' Committee, had called student athletic trainers "the backbone of the college training room." He said, "Primarily student athletic trainers use the internship to gain hours of exposure toward certification as an athletic trainer."

In response to the question a few years later, Newman predicted removal of the internship option would have an impact, but ultimately a beneficial one. He said:

> Initially, we may see a smaller number of students coming out, but the quality of those students who come out will dramatically increase. And long-term, I think as we, as a profession, become more widely recognized and more opportunities open up, then we're going to have a more qualified entry-level athletic trainer.

5

THE JOURNAL

Nurturing a Seven-Year-Old

Not surprisingly, the periodical literature of sports medicine before NATA's formation had few citations relating to athletic training.

There was the *Trainers Journal*, billed as the "Official Publication of the National Athletic Trainers Association" that was founded before World War II. Inserted as a section of a publication called *The Athletic Journal*, it provided some of the earliest descriptions of a profession in its infancy.

About the same time, Collett Publishing in Fort Worth was circulating a national magazine called *The Mentor*. It described its audience as "coaches, trainers and sportsmen."

Then there were two publications disseminated by the Cramer Chemical Co., the Gardner, KS godfather of athletic training. Although they had no pretensions of being scholarly publications, *The Trainer* and *The First Aider* had articles on treatment and techniques and enjoyed substantial readership among athletic trainers.

In a trade that aspired to be a profession, there was clearly a need for a scholarly journal, and NATA was supposed to provide it. The Association did—eventually.

In NATA's seventh year, the time was ripe, and the *NATA Journal* made its debut in September 1956. A caveat in the masthead proclaimed: "Original writings or works cited in the *Journal*

does not [sic] necessarily represent the positions of the Association or its Board of Directors."

The editor, Arthur L. Dickinson, Arizona State University, was not one to overpromise. He said, "The editors of *Life,* the *Journal of the American Medical Association,* the *Research Quarterly* will not sit up until the silly hours of the morning worrying about the competition."

Nor did he minimize the need for the publication. In that first issue, he wrote:

> First, there is a need for an exchange of ideas and techniques. A profession that pauses to sit down may as well lay down, for it is a dead profession.
>
> Second, the *Journal* will be able to disseminate information of professional interest to the athletic trainer from a multitude of sources.
>
> Third, the professional stature of the organization can be raised through written contributions from every member; along with the value of this material to himself and his fellow members, it can help to inform the public and the profession we are allied with of the importance of athletic training. We owe it to ourselves and to the coming generation of men to grow enough to insure proper and adequate care for the health and safety of everyone who chooses to participate in high school, college or professional athletics.

Dickinson wasted no time before editorializing on the responsibility of the members. In that first issue, he noted that the Association was now seven years old, and he declared, "It is high time that each member took it upon himself to improve the Association as whole. This we can do by becoming salesmen extraordinaire."

He went on to say athletic trainers needed to sell the value of the profession to high school and college administrators and the public. "Before we can be recognized by the medical profession," he said, "our job is to prove by our progress and our work that we are justly deserving. This will be a selling job where no one may fall short, or we shall all fail."

As a new publication supported by limited resources, the *Journal* was spartan in size and appearance. When it appeared the following April, it had 16 pages, four-and-a-half of which were advertising. The issue for the next quarter was published on glossy stock. There would be improvements, and they were going to be incremental.

Under Dickinson's direction, the *Journal* menu served articles like "Approach to Low Back Problems With Relationship to Foot Balance," Joseph Doller, author. There were book reviews and listings of periodical literature of interest. To beef up the editorial content, the Board decided in 1958 that each director should contribute an article in each issue. With nine members on the Board at the time, that output, had it ever materialized, would have surpassed the number of available pages.

Dickinson edited the *Journal* until 1959, when he was replaced by Jackie Copeland, Odessa (TX) High School.

If the early *Journals* lacked the scientific content that readers would ultimately come to expect, they still managed to evoke interest. An example was the hot questions and their responses described in Jimmy H. Railey's 1963 article reporting a shoe-string survey of coaches. Did coaches abide by the head trainer's decision to hold an injured player out of a practice or game? "Always," replied 97 percent of the coaches. Were head trainers doing their jobs well? All yesses on that one. Are trainers properly prepared to carry out their duties? Only 3 percent thought they weren't.

The December 1964 issue was characterized by change. The editor's responsibilities had been split up. D. Conrad Jarvis, Stanford University, was the editor, and he doubled as the ad manager. There was also a managing editor, Marvin Roberson, Foothill College.

That issue was also the first to use pictures—black-and-white photos taken at the annual meeting. Another first was the use of photography on the cover.

By the spring 1968 issue, the *Journal* had progressed to 24 pages, 13 of which were advertising. A new section, classified ads for jobs, appeared in this issue. A well-intended but unworkable idea, this feature was gone by the summer issue. The long interval between issues made publication of job searches and announcements impractical.

At the annual meeting in 1968, the Board was looking for ways to communicate better with the membership and instructed the executive director to write a column every quarter. In one of his final acts as executive director, Pinky Newell wrote the first column. He chose a subject sure to capture reader interest—the need to raise the dues.

The early editors were engaged in an ongoing struggle so characteristic of the publishing business in general: finding good material. Clyde Stretch, Michigan State University, who was assistant editor at the time, expressed his dismay in one column:

> Our *Journal* editor [he was referring to Marvin Roberson], in the last newsletter for the American College of Sports Medicine, asked that organization's membership for articles that might be placed in our *Journal.* This would seem to be a sad reflection on our membership. Why should our editor have to look elsewhere for material? . . . We cannot, nor should we have to, depend on any other group to supply material for our own publication.

As the 1960s came to an end, the *Journal* was concluding its fledgling years, having acquired the feathers necessary to fly. The Board seemed to regard the publication as viable, but there was still plenty of work to do. At the 1969 annual meeting in Cincinnati, the Board appointed a special committee and charged it with improving the *Journal* and giving it a more professional format.

The Tectonic Period

The early 1970s found NATA undergoing the re-engineering called the Reorganization Plan. This remodeling of the NATA house would also affect the architecture of all its wings and ells. Including the *Journal.*

The Board was now meeting twice a year. The *Journal* began publishing verbatim, and in very small type that invited eyestrain, the "Proceedings of the Annual Business Meeting" as well as the minutes of the annual and midyear Board meetings.

Readers of the March 1972 issue noticed a few changes. For one thing, it had a new look, and it was going from a quarterly to six times a year—a frequency that was to be short lived. Abstracts of articles pertinent to athletic training were introduced. Also, the publication had a new name. It was now *Athletic Training*—the Journal of the National Athletic Trainers' Association.

Another thing about that redesigned issue—it was late. The editor was direct in his assessment of the woes of a publication makeover. "Minor difficulties," he wrote, "began to pile up rapidly enough that what were normally minor hurdles suddenly became major ones, and the final product in terms of delay in publication resulted in a two-and-a-half-month disaster."

Late delivery was a recurring problem for editors, who were at the mercy of the printer. Clint Thompson, editor in the '70s and '80s, recalled:

> If there were any late *Journals,* and unfortunately there were some in those days, it was almost exclusively because the publisher didn't get them out on time. . . . It would be interesting to see how many publishing companies we have gone through, because a number of those were discarded because of their poor efficiency.

Although management of the *Journal* resided with the editors, oversight of the publication was in the hands of the Journal Committee. In 1973, Committee members were also responsible for producing the various departments or columns appearing in the *Journal.*

The *Journal* editors by the mid-70s were using black-and-white photography generously, usually to illustrate treatments and techniques. On a couple of occasions, the objective was to shock. Inserted in the September 1974 issue was a tear-out poster which could be displayed on the training room wall.

KENNETH KNIGHT

During his tenure as editor and later editor-in-chief from 1985 through 1996, Ken Knight presided over a lot of changes designed to make a better *Journal.*

One change he didn't want to see, however, was moving the *Journal* editorial office from Indiana State, his school, to Dallas as a cost-cutting measure. When he went one Sunday to meet with the NATA Finance Committee to oppose the move, he found it was a done deal. "That," he said, "was known as Black Sunday among the *Journal* Committee." But he persuaded the Finance Committee to revisit the issue. A former president of the Council of Biology Editors was retained as a consultant. After investigation, the advice was that the *Journal* was worth more—not less—money, so let's find it. The Board agreed.

Knight concentrated his efforts on making the *Journal* a more scholarly publication and improving the quality of the writing. He also pressed printers to overcome a problem that had bedeviled earlier editors—getting the publication out on time. In retrospect, he said, "I think we went a long ways with the *Journal.*"

CLINT THOMPSON

Clint Thompson was at Colorado State in 1970 when he began working on the *Journal*, and in two years he would become editor. More than a quarter of a century later, when NATA celebrated its 50th anniversary, he was still at work on the *Journal*, the longest span of service for anyone associated with that publication.

In the early days, it was pretty much of a two-man operation. Thompson recalled:

Rod Compton was editor-in-chief in those days, and he more or less carried the ball with the Board of Directors. And I handled the daily workings of soliciting articles, reviewing articles and that kind of thing. The biggest thing was trying to secure quality articles. I think I'd say it was quasi successful. The *Journal* has changed a lot. It's a lot better now than it used to be. The professionalism of the articles you see in today's *Journal* is a step or two above what we used to get. That was probably my biggest challenge.

For the *Journal* editors, service had to be a labor of love. For Thompson, that meant about five to ten hours a week dispatching authors' articles he had received—first to reviewers, then back to the authors for revision and then, after checking the revisions, off to the printer.

"None of the things that happened on my watch were earth-shaking," opined Thompson. "But there were a lot of things that if you put them all together, they made the *Journal* a better *Journal*."

The photography, of the head-on collision genre, supported the headline: "Two Good Reasons to Wear Your Mouth Guard." Three years later the poster was re-run. Explained Editor-in-Chief Rod Compton, "It may be a little hard-hitting, but it has been very effective in getting athletes to wear their mouth guards."

The publication's quality, particularly in terms of content, continued to improve. By the mid-70s, there was no dearth of material, and the editors could afford to be choosy about what they printed. There was an Editorial Review Board, the function of which, explained Thompson, was "to assure that when an article appears in the *Journal*, it meets the high standards for which NATA stands." After receiving the Review Board's evaluation, it was up to the editors to accept, reject or return the manuscript to the author for revision. When the editor was sold on the submission, it was forwarded to the editor-in-chief for publication.

Aside from a common quest for superlative material and a receptive readership, editors had their individual causes and aspirations for the publication. Rod Compton's wish list included making the *Journal* a reference staple in libraries. But less than 2 percent of U.S. libraries were carrying the publication, he lamented in a 1975 editorial. He urged readers to contact local and university libraries about installing the athletic training quarterly so it would be available to medical personnel and students.

Mary Edgerly was appointed managing editor in 1977, and her salary was to be paid from advertising. A year later, Otho Davis, in his executive director's report to the annual meeting, congratulated her, and for a very good reason. For the first time, the *Journal* had turned a profit!

To "promote scholarship among young athletic trainers," the *Journal* announced an annual Student Writing Contest in 1978. In addition to a $100 cash award, the winner would see his or her article in print. The first winner was Lori Ames Galstad, a student athletic trainer at the University of Wisconsin-LaCrosse. Her article, "Anterior Tibial

Compartment Syndrome," appeared in the fall 1979 issue.

Regularly running 72 pages, the publication in the 1980s was filled with academic articles, case histories and helpful departments such as "Tips From the Field." By the time Ken Wolfert, Miami (Ohio) University, was editor-in-chief, the problem of attracting sufficient items to fill the space had been reversed. In fact, he wrote in 1983: "The time has come to seriously consider what to do with the large amount of materials we have available for publication. There is more copy to print than ever before."

He suggested that NATA should consider publishing a companion "newsletter" to absorb some of the features that were being squeezed in the *Journal.* Before the decade ended, he would get his wish.

Kenneth Knight, Indiana State University, became editor in 1986. He faced two challenges in improving the *Journal,* one of which was to restrict the publication to scholarly content by removing the material related to Association business. "It took us four or five years before we could convince the leadership that it needed to be done," he said.

His second challenge was to improve the quality of the writing. "Most of my authors were not polished writers, and we worked a great deal at editing and working with people to try to improve their presentation of some very good information," he explained.

The NATA News

As one reader complained in a letter to the editor, the reason *Journal* articles were never listed in the *Index Medicus* and other periodical indices was that NATA's quarterly contained too many non-scholarly departments that belonged somewhere else.

The solution was the one Wolfert and Knight had suggested. In the fall of 1988, it appeared: Vol. 1, No. 1 of the "Newsletter of the National Athletic Trainers Association." The editor was John LeGear of the Association's public relations agency

at the time, and he was open to suggestions for a permanent name for the publication. It became the *NATA News,* a publication which would be the sole vehicle for communicating Association business to the members. The research, literature reviews and in-depth techniques articles would remain with the *Journal.*

In its first ten years, the *NATA News* would, like the *Journal,* make changes and improvements incrementally. Frequency of publication was changed to monthly in 1992. Redesigned at the beginning of 1998, the *NATA News* was running 44 pages, and the publication was graphically appealing, thanks partly to generous use of full color.

Pot Holes on the Freeway

In the journalism fraternity, there is a proverb: *Doctors bury their mistakes; editors and writers publish theirs for all to see.* The achievements of the *Journal* editors were not made without bumping up against that truth.

Rod Compton reminded readers in 1975 that the *Journal* was produced by volunteers; the editors, the Journal Committee and the Editorial Review Board devoted a lot of time without compensation. "This is even more remarkable considering how busy their professional positions keep them without this additional labor of love," he wrote.

Chafing at comments made during a Board meeting, he later wrote:

> It does seem quite sad that all that was said about the *Journal* was " . . . as usual, it was getting out late." I sincerely believe that if any complaining member[s] had to be responsible for one or two issues of the *Journal,* that he or she would realize how difficult the project is and still maintain their full-time position of trainer.

Undoubtedly, there were times the editors regretted the letters column that enabled readers to vent. A 1980 ad for dimethyl sulfoxide, not yet approved by the FDA for human use, brought eight letters of rebuke. Huffed one reader: "I thought that NATA, along with the NCAA, has taken a stand against the use of ergogenic aids of any kind to attempt to increase one's athletic performance."

The publishing of a crossword puzzle in 1989 provoked complaints from two readers. One opined "the inclusion of such things as this in a scholarly journal gives rise to unwanted and unneeded criticism."

Nor was the Board immune to flack. In early 1992, the Board decided to discontinue student subscriptions to the *Journal.* The ensuing protests convinced the directors to reverse themselves at the annual meeting in June.

But consciously or not, the editors found that criticism, when offered constructively, could be a valuable asset. Often it helped keep them and others associated with the publication to stay focused enough to successfully navigate a difficult expressway.

Toward a More Scholarly Journal

The inception of the *NATA News* enabled the *Journal* staff to restrict its content to research and academic work and thereby reshuffle editorial responsibilities. The editor position was eliminated in 1991, and Knight became editor-in-chief. When he retired in 1996, after many years with the *Journal,* the publication he had supervised was frequently a robust 96 pages.

One of the changes during Knight's tenure was a new title for the publication. It had been *Athletic Training* since 1972. In January 1992, the nameplate read *Journal of Athletic Training.*

Knight's successor, David Perrin, spelled out his plans for the *Journal,* or *JAT,* in his first issue:

In a broad sense, my goal for the *Journal of Athletic Training* is to place it in the best possible position for acceptance by the leading medical indexes. Toward that end I will enhance its scholarly image, both in appearance and in content.

We'll also encourage other members of the sports medicine community to consider *JAT* as a forum for their writing. I want the *Journal of Athletic Training* to be the periodical of choice for both publication and discussion for all professionals involved in the health care of physically active people.

Journal articles were indexed in literature indices such as *SPORT Discus* and *Focus on Sports Science & Medicine.* But NATA editors going back to Rod Compton had coveted the recognition for the *Journal* and its editors that could be attained in listings of the *Index Medicus.* Perrin, too, shared this aspiration. In an editorial titled "Toward a More Scholarly Journal," he wrote:

. . . consider a student who conducts an *Index Medicus* literature search in the health sciences library for a class writing assignment. What is the message if the student finds articles from several other sports medicine and allied health-care journals but fails to find any from *JAT*? And what is the message if the student builds his or her reference list for the paper with very few articles from *JAT*? A high-quality journal can help attract the top students to our profession.

Journal progress over the years has been steady, if not dramatic. Clint Thompson, a fixture with the publication for so many years, observed: "There was nothing that jumped out [at any one time] to say it really set the world on fire. Ever since 1956, it has been a piecemeal improvement."

But over time most of the pieces have been put in place, and aspirations for esteemed indexing and other recognition no longer seem so remote. If they could only glimpse the then-and-now contrast of the publication they helped create, Arthur Dickinson and his early successors could easily be afflicted with an un-editorlike impairment—a loss of words with which to express their astonishment.

The Journal Editors

Arthur L. Dickinson,
Arizona State U., editor 1956–59

Jackie Copeland,
Odessa (TX) High School, editor 1959–64

D. Conrad Jarvis,
Stanford U., editor 1964–67

Marvin Roberson,
Foothill College *et al,* managing ed. 1964,
editor 1967–72

Clyde Stretch,
Michigan State U., assistant ed. 1967,
editor-in-chief 1972–73

Clinton Thompson,
Colorado State U., editor 1972–84

Rod Compton,
East Carolina State U., editor-in-chief 1973–79

Ken Wolfert,
Miami (OH) U., editor-in-chief 1979–83

Steve Yates,
Wake Forest U., editor-in-chief 1983–91

Don Kaverman,
Ferris State College, editor 1984–86

Ken Knight,
Indiana State U., editor 1986, editor-in-chief 1991–96

David Perrin,
University of Virginia, editor-in-chief 1996–

6

COLLABORATION AND CONTENTION: INTRA-PROFESSION RELATIONS

The District Associations

Sports medicine is a diverse profession with each interest fragment represented in some fashion. The athletic training component operates as a federation of districts which are independent in matters within their territories but at the same time are integrated nationally into the whole, which is NATA. And then there are the state organizations and the associations representing athletic trainers in professional sports.

Mindful of the regional parochialism that contributed to the failure of the first national association, NATA founders wanted to build the Association on a strong grass-roots foundation. Nine district athletic trainers' associations were formed to align with the several regional associations that had been in place beginning with the 1946 founding of the Southeastern Athletic Trainers Association. Within the confines of their own turf, the districts would operate independent of NATA, choosing their own officers, crafting their own agendas and bylaws. They would also elect district directors who would constitute the NATA Board of Directors.

Among the district officers were secretaries who had a number of duties relating to NATA. Since district members were also NATA members, the district secretaries collected the dues for both

organizations. They were also supposed to contribute four articles for the *Journal* each year.

James "Doc" Dodson, secretary of District 6 going back to 1967, fondly remembered the give and take of early dues collecting:

> Well, Pinky [Newell] would call and say, "When are you going to get your dues money in?" And I'd say, "When is it supposed to be in?" And we'd jaw back and forth because we were trying to draw the little bit of money that we had—the interest on that money—and we would keep it as long as we could. So, when Pinky said, "Well, you need to have it in on the first of October, or the first of November," well, then I would cut him a check and send it right off to him. And Pinky was such a pleasant person to work with.

Such informality was apparently typical of the early district organizations. Except perhaps for the older, entrenched associations, they seemed unstructured and in search of a mission for serving their local constituencies.

Their function as part of a two-way conduit to transmit the will of the membership to the national organization and national policy back to the hustings was not immediately realized. Initially, most of the districts were holding their meetings only at NATA's annual conference. As late as 1968, Pinky Newell was chiding the districts for not holding separate meetings back home. Failure to do so, he feared, would leave members who didn't attend the NATA meetings out of the loop.

Jack Rockwell expressed dismay at how things worked when he was a district director on the Board: "They had district secretaries' meetings at the National, when they would get together like the Board of Directors, and they kind of ran things in some areas . . . I was rather shocked to find that the district secretaries were almost, and in some cases, more powerful than the Board of Directors."

If the district secretaries had clout, it was because they earned it. They were to the early NATA what worker bees are to the hive. Frank George, NATA president from 1974–78, considered the district secretaries to be essentially the Association's national staff.

> It was the district secretaries who really ran the business end of the Association. They determined who were members, they determined who was up on their dues, not up on their dues. . . . The 10 district secretaries were very busy people. . . . We could not have gotten along without them.

Like NATA, the district organizations were operated totally by volunteers in basically uncharted territory, and like NATA, they were groping for programs of substance to help define what they were all about.

NATA and the districts achieved their quest at about the same time. Much of the impetus for this was furnished by the NATA reorganization of the early 1970s. The National Association was now situated to expand programs and services, particularly in athletic training education. Seizing their opportunity, the districts began initiatives of their own to supplement NATA programs at the local level.

Soon there would be district meetings. One of the earliest was inaugurated in 1976 by District 9, which represented athletic trainers in the Southeast. A dozen years later that organization would be sponsoring meetings for student athletic trainers.

NATA's involvement with education and research was emulated by the districts. Several hundred athletic trainers would come to owe at least part of their education to district scholarships.

Numerous research papers were underwritten by district grants. Since district meetings were also venues for athletic training workshops, they offered opportunities for continuing education, and District 6 began in 1995 verifying CEUs earned by registrants.

Possibly the clearest example of district leadership in enhancing the profession is found in the issue of licensure. Beginning with District 6's successful effort to persuade the Texas legislature in 1971 to license athletic trainers, such regulation has had high priority among the districts. In the name of raising the bar for the quality of athletes' care, lobbying by the districts has produced licensure or some form of regulation in most states. In some cases, the legislatures enacted statutes that have not withstood the test of time, and the quest for improvement is an on-going topic for the district organizations.

Another district issue is the 40-plus states where athletic trainers have formed their own associations. These state associations operate independently of the districts. Many district leaders support the concept of state organizations, viewing them as a means of improving communication with their own members and as allies on many local issues. Others say they are not so enthusiastic about organizing the profession below the district level.

The significant strides made by the district groups after 1970 were in keeping with the vision NATA's founders had in setting up the district organizations. In 1988, NATA developed a 90-minute symposium, "Athletic Training in the '90s," to present its goals and strategies for the following decade. Sponsored by Johnson & Johnson, the symposium was held at district meetings because of their ability to draw so many members. President Jerry Rhea described the town meeting-type format as "an exciting open forum of ideas. We're probably learning more from our members than they're learning from us."

A survey of district directors and secretaries in 1998 revealed a highly homogeneous agenda of concerns for the present and the near future:

• Third-party reimbursement

- Promulgating public recognition of the indispensability of the athletic trainer
- Closer unification of the various practice settings
- Improving licensing statutes
- Expanding employment opportunities for athletic trainers with compensation commensurate with the value of their service

As the embodiment of its ten constituencies, NATA also had these concerns—as well as some funds—to do something about them. In 1996, for example, the National Association allocated $300,000 to the districts for use in state regulatory and reimbursement activities.

Athletic Trainers and Professional Sports

When NATA was organized in 1950, there were 16 Major League baseball teams, all of them still operating in the same cities where they played ball at the beginning of the 20th Century. When the Braves left Boston in 1953 for Milwaukee, on the way to Atlanta, it signaled the beginning of a new era of not only relocation but expansion. New franchises for basketball, football and hockey were not far behind. In the aftermath of World War II, the public had developed an appetite for professional sports. Good times for the national economy had given them the money to feed it.

NATA's charter members primarily practiced in colleges and in some high schools—the traditional setting. Perhaps some of them were prescient enough to see what was about to take place in spectator sports; but in any event, they recognized that they had much in common with the athletic trainers who ministered to the pros. In 1952, the Board opened membership to the athletic trainers in professional sports.

Life for the pro team athletic trainers was different in many ways, however. For one thing, they had longer seasons, and they were away from home much of the time. They were looking for organizations that could focus on their specific needs. In 1972, the National Basketball Trainers

Association was formed. The next decade would see the arrival of the Ps—the Professional Baseball Athletic Trainers Society (PBATS), PFATS (football) and PHATS (hockey).

Jack Rockwell, employed during the 1960s by the St. Louis Cardinals football team, remembers the spadework that led to PFATS:

> We tried for two or three years to get things going, and finally I went to New York and talked to Commissioner Roselle. The first question Pete asked me, "What do you want to do? Why are you trying to do this?" And I said, "I want to get the people together." I said, "We never see each other. We see each other on the field on Sunday, and that's not good enough. We want to exchange ideas, talk." He says, "You're not going to form a union, are you?" And, of course, that was right at the height of the union problems in the National Football League. And I said, "No, no." "Well," he says, "if you do, we'll fire you." And I believe he would have.

The pro team associations set up their own foundations and programs. PBATS is an example. Together with team physicians, the baseball team athletic trainers have co-sponsored a baseball medicine conference that dates back to 1985. And PBATS has taken aim at a controversy in the institution of baseball—spit tobacco—joining other groups in a program to educate athletes, particularly younger ones, on the insidious downside of the habit, notably periodontal disease, leukoplakia and oral cancer.

Despite their independent purviews, the professional team groups and NATA pursue many shared interests together. There is a crossover in memberships, and historically a large proportion of NATA presidents have come from the ranks of the professional team athletic trainers.

Even in the best of families, tensions sometimes arise. Again, PBATS furnishes the example. In NATA participation, the baseball team athletic trainers are at a disadvantage compared with their brethren in other sports. The June annual meetings of NATA get sparse attendance from the 200 or so (in 1998) baseball athletic trainers who are in the midst of their seasons. But if there is a will, there is

Kent Biggerstaff (R), PBATS president and head athletic trainer for the Pittsburgh Pirates, works with fellow certified athletic trainer Bill Henry and intern Jamie Wolf.

a way to work together. This can be illustrated by another PBATS activity, a summer internship program for student athletic trainers. (A PBATS program, but publicized by NATA.)

Treating Olympians

The Olympic Games have long held a special meaning for athletic trainers. To be selected as an athletic trainer for the U.S. Olympic team is a coveted honor. Moreover, it has always been a valuable experience. Long before the founding of NATA, the Games represented a world classroom of sorts where learning exchange took place. Having the opportunity to meet peers from all points of the compass and pass along and receive unfamiliar but valuable techniques for treating athletes—now for most athletic trainers that is an opportunity to die for.

Selection of athletic trainers for the Olympics and the Pan American Games was originally through NATA, which had set up a committee for that purpose. Athletic trainers would apply through their respective districts, which would submit nominees to the Association's Olympic Selection Committee. For an athletic trainer to go around the process and solicit appointment directly from the

Athletic trainers for the 1968 United States Olympic Team.

Almost 800 certified athletic trainers volunteered for the 1996 Olympic Games in Atlanta. Shown are some of the ATCs who participated in the Opening Ceremonies.

U.S. Olympic Committee was a breach of NATA's Code of Ethics.

For some time, NATA attempted to work out an agreement with USOC on the selection process. Frustrated with the lack of progress, NATA's Board in 1978 voted to take the Association out of the selection business. Athletic trainers were now free to solicit Olympics' appointments on their own.

An interesting footnote to the international sports competitions was a political rumble in which American athletic trainers were invited to take part. As Cold War tensions created rivalries that included sports, the eyebrow-raising performances of Eastern Bloc athletes, notably from the Soviet Union and East Germany, caused consternation among observers associated with U.S. Olympic programs and other Free World competitors. Was it something the record-breaking East Bloc athletes were eating for breakfast?

"Or do they have training secrets we don't possess?" Ernest B. McCoy wondered aloud during his speech at NATA's 1959 annual meeting. McCoy, athletic director at Penn State, issued a challenge to NATA members:

> Gentlemen, perhaps it may be possible through experimentation and research to find a partial substitute for the regimented and professional approach of the Russians for success in athletic achievement. We must find a way! And we need your help to find the answer!

World politics aside, over the years NATA and USOC have found common cause in a number of areas. One of these was an annual seminar co-sponsored by the two organizations and the Sports Physical Therapy Section of the American Physical Therapy Association. The series was introduced in 1995 in Birmingham, the topic being "Closed Kinetic Chain in Sports Rehabilitation: Scientific Basis and Functional Application."

Brothers of the Lodge: ATCs and PTs

Athletic trainers and physical therapists—if they're not siblings, they're at least kissin' cousins. Many ATCs also sport the certification credentials of the American Physical Therapy Association. The two organizations, NATA and APTA, have collaborated on many issues of mutual interest over the years.

Certainly among close-knit kin it would take a highly charged issue to provoke a dispute. The migration of many athletic trainers into clinical and industrial settings was just such an issue.

APTA issued a statement in 1988 purportedly to clarify who does what and who reports to whom:

> As you can see, the working roles of the two organizations [NATA and APTA] overlap in their basic philosophies. The NATA's philosophies are directed at athletic care in the school/college/ university setting, the amateur organization setting, and the professional organization setting. The traditional team concept places the team physician and supervisor with the ATC treating athletes from *only that team or organization.* There is no fee for service, no third-party payers, and it is not called physical therapy. The Sports Physical Therapist may treat on referral or direct access [as directed by his or her physical therapy practice act] athletes *from all walks of life and with all types of medical background* in hospital, clinic and training room environments. In the traditional team concept setting, the Sports PT would interact with the athlete at the trainer's or physician's request.
>
> . . . Clinical settings providing physical therapy services which employ an ATC must provide that the ATC functions under the direct supervision of the physical therapist.

Kenneth L. Knight, editor of the *Journal,* commented on the statement: "Some athletic trainers are upset by this document because they feel it is a putdown of the athletic training profession. Others feel it applies only to athletic trainers and physical therapists who work in sports medicine clinics and that it was long overdue."

There was an open wound, and it was festering. In 1990, the two associations formed a joint task force, and for the better part of two years they worked to resolve practice issues. The task force developed a list of recommendations, but to no avail. In 1991, President Mark Smaha announced that the Board had rejected the recommendations as not being in the best interests of NATA. The task force was disbanded.

The disagreement was shelved as the two organizations looked for areas in which they were more compatible. In 1995 and 1998, the Sports Physical Therapy Section of APTA, along with the U.S. Olympic Committee, would be co-sponsors of NATA's Sports Medicine Seminar.

American Athletic Trainers Association

NATA's relations with a California-based association representing athletic trainers warrants an historical footnote. It centers on a single adversarial incident.

In 1992, the American Athletic Trainers Association was found to be appropriating for its own members' use some valuable NATA property, namely the ATC designation. NATA and the NATABOC filed suit, charging infringement on the federally registered mark.

The court ruled in NATA's favor, and AATA agreed to cease and desist. When AATA violated the agreement, it was cited for contempt. Ultimately, NATA was awarded $25,000, and its certification mark was preserved.

7

BIG ISSUES, ADROIT STRATEGIES

Recognition of the Athletic Trainer, "Friend of Mankind"

If everyone had Walter Stewart's appreciation for athletic training, NATA's directors could have dispensed with their Board meetings and gone home.

In the mid-1950s, sports columnist Stewart asserted in the *Memphis Commercial Appeal* that "the trainer, for the most part, works in strict anonymity. Unless he is dredged for information concerning the status of a knee belonging to Marty McMuscle, the peerless fullback, his name never reaches the printed page except as the last item in the football brochure . . . but a college team would be a rudderless barge without him."

After describing the significant but uncelebrated role of the athletic trainer, Stewart concluded his article, "Hail to the trainer, friend of mankind."

Since most people are not privy to such insight, NATA Boards from Day One have grappled with the task of obtaining public and professional recognition for athletic training. Without it, there would be no acceptance, no viable profession. For 50 years, many strategies would be developed and implemented. There would be internal strategies developed to raise the competence level of athletic training through education and research. Externally, the Association would rely on gathering data that supported the profession and public relations to disseminate the information convincingly.

If it is true that a problem well stated is a problem half solved, NATA at its founding wasn't even close. Athletic trainers simply weren't sure who they were, whose camp they were in. At the 1954 annual meeting, Board Chairman Thomas "Fitz" Lutz gave his opinion:

> You have heard rumors in the convention about the NCAA, and they have kinda winked at us . . . so we have appointed [Pinky Newell, Purdue; Millard Kelly, College of the Pacific; and Dr. Robert G. Brashear, University of Tennessee] to investigate and see if there is a possibility of us being admitted to one of the accredited medical associations. I think this is the way we should do it—not with the coaches. We lean to the medical and not to coaching.

And that direction, attempting to win recognition from the medical community, was the course NATA set off on.

An early sign of acceptance came in 1959. At the annual meeting that year, members were told that NATA had been recognized by the American College Health Association. There would also be similar acknowledgments by other groups ranging from the American Physical Therapy Association to the U.S. Field and Track Federation.

But June 22, 1967 was the big red-letter day for NATA and athletic training. In a telegram to Pinky Newell, Fred V. Hein, director of health education for the American Medical Association, announced an AMA resolution. It stated that AMA recognized the professionally prepared athletic trainer as part of the team responsible for the athletes' care. It commended NATA for its efforts to upgrade standards of the profession. And it encouraged state and local medical societies and physicians individually to help advance NATA's professional goals through appropriate liaison activities.

Arriving on Pinky's 47th birthday, the telegram was undoubtedly the best present he could have received. It marked the first step in securing AMA endorsement of athletic training, and he had doggedly pursued it with the medical society for almost 13 years.

Once NATA became a certification body, recognition entered a second phase. By 1983, the Association had gained Regular Category A membership in the National Commission of Health Certifying Agencies. In making the announcement, NATA President Bobby Barton credited Gary Craner, Boise State University, with the idea for membership; Dr. Gerald Bell, University of Illinois, with the initial investigation; and Paul Grace, Massachusetts Institute of Technology, with making the application and representing NATA at hearings.

Then came the fruition of an initiative that began in the 1970s—AMA accreditation of the Association's education program. As chairman of the Professional Education Committee, Robert S. Behnke had revived the effort in 1987. On June 22, 1990, the ship came in. NATA had received the coveted stamp of approval of the AMA committee that would later be known as the Commission on Accreditation of Allied Health Education Programs (CAAHEP). Simply put, athletic training was now fully recognized by AMA as an allied health-care profession.

Several factors contributed to the realization of Fitz Lutz's vision that NATA leaders embraced. NATA persistence in knocking at the door. NATA's

measures to raise the professional competence of athletic training, removed insufficient preparation as justification for footdragging. But there were also external circumstances that worked in NATA's favor, too. Afraid of being sued, many doctors wanted out of sports activities—let the athletic trainers do it. Also, in rural areas, there weren't enough doctors to handle normal patient loads, let alone sports injuries.

High School Athletes at Risk

In August 1998, a letter published in *USA Today* called the deaths of two Kansas high school football players "a wakeup call to school administrators." The writer, athletic trainer Jeff Bray, pointed to athletic trainer ratios: one for every 25 colleges and professional athletes, but only one for every 5,000 athletes in high school. He wrote:

> Although a physician or certified athletic trainer cannot prevent all injuries or deaths resulting from participation in athletics, reducing the risks is the obligation of those sponsoring the activity.
>
> The parents of the young men who died playing the game that is the dream of American youth say they don't place blame. But I must question the priorities of those sponsoring the activity.
>
> If school districts feel they cannot justify the full-time employment of a qualified health-care professional, can they justify letting students play the game?

Nine paragraphs in the largest circulation daily newspaper in the U.S. were a free publicity windfall supporting a longtime NATA goal: persuading school districts to hire athletic trainers.

Actually, school administrators were only one obstacle. They had their own problems in wringing out enough money from often lean budgets to pay teachers and heat the classrooms.

The general public had to be the main target. They were the taxpayers who, theoretically at least, influenced school boards.

NATA's interest was undeniably self-serving. With the number of athletic trainers swelling, where were the jobs for them? Secondary schools represented a fertile employment market. But the public had an important stake, too. They were parents, and many of them had children playing middle school and high school sports. The number of injuries suffered by their kids demanded action.

Consequently, the strategy adopted by NATA leaders was to show the public the issue in terms of their own self-interest. The tactics were to gather evidence of the problem through research and then employ an intensive public relations push to disseminate the compelling findings.

There had been early efforts. In 1971, Kendall Sports Division had produced a film for NATA. Titled *The Absent Link*, the film indicated that athletic trainers—the link between the team physicians and the coaching staff—were unlikely to be found at secondary schools. The 29-minute film story was intended to convince parents and school administrators of the need to employ athletic trainers in their school districts and encourage young men to consider athletic training as a career choice.

Help from Congress was also explored. In 1973, Ronald Dellums, a Congressman from California, introduced a bill known as the Athletic Care Act. It would require all secondary schools and colleges sponsoring intercollegiate sports to have a certified athletic trainer.

The Dellums bill sounded good to NATA's Board, which voted to endorse it. But when that action was reported at the annual membership meeting, "that's when it exploded," remembered Frank George, who had supported the bill. Some members saw it as just more unwanted government intervention. And despite the fact that the bill proposed to stretch out incrementally compliance over a period of time, many members feared there wouldn't be enough athletic trainers to supply all the schools.

The Dellums bill died. Too bad, many members lamented even years later. One NATA leader, considering the profession's employment concerns, ruefully predicted, "That particular bill would have answered all our problems today."

So, the question persisted, How best to reach and influence parents of the estimated 20 million students enrolled in junior and senior high schools? The answer was to be the National High School Injury Registry (NHSIR). Adopted by NATA in 1985, NHSIR was underwritten by Johnson & Johnson and Gatorade/Quaker Oats. It would measure the rate and severity of high school sports injuries.

An Oak Park, IL, public relations agency, Timothy Communications, was retained to disseminate the NHSIR findings via TV and radio public service announcements and media press releases.

In 1987, Dr. John Powell, NHSIR director, had the facts. The survey of 105 high schools projected 636,000 injuries nationally in high school football, 62 percent of them being sustained in practice. He announced the results at a press conference in New York which produced stories in such illustrious media outlets as the "Today Show," CNN and *USA Today.*

The NHSIR study was concluded, temporarily at least, in 1989. NATA Executive Director Otho Davis explained: "We've demonstrated to the public that injuries are a crucial factor in sports that must be addressed. There is evidence that more school administrators are addressing the problem. We'll shift our emphasis now to provide recommendations for solutions to the problem."

By 1995, NHSIR was back in business. In reinstating the program, NATA added other sports to football, basketball and wrestling that were tracked in the earlier study. When findings of the football portion of the survey were announced the following year at a Dallas press conference, the number of projected injuries had dropped somewhat to 506,452, which was still something not to be dismissed lightly. Again, about two-thirds of those injuries were occurring in practice.

On the occasion of NATA's golden jubilee, the issue of athletic trainers in high schools was far from a wrap. In the minds of many, progress had been frustratingly slow. Jack Rockwell observed: "We've never been able to penetrate the high school level with athletic trainers, not to the extent that I feel we should. I mean, we're much less than 10 percent of the high schools covered in the United States. It's only in recent years that we've covered the junior colleges."

For both athletic trainers and the school administrators, it's a stubborn pocketbook issue. This was recognized by many NATA leaders, including Marjorie Albohm. She said: "Economics will always be an issue, regardless of what profession we're talking about, for the public schools." She envisioned NATA's proper role as offering athletic trainers a tool box of things to enhance their employment opportunities.

> . . . but it comes down to you personally using those tools and taking the initiative to say to your administration, to your coaches, to your community, your parents, your school board, the people who you directly help, whose children's lives you affect, to say, "I'm a valuable entity to you. This is what I do. This is how I help you. This is why I'm important." And that has to start with each of us.

License to Practice

There was a day when just anyone could practice athletic training. And when anyone, regardless of competence, can do that, the reputation of the rest of the profession is at risk. Leaders in the profession, from NATA on down to the state organizations, understood this threat and what was needed to eliminate or minimize it—licensure.

District 6 was the first to strike oil—in Texas, naturally. Assenting to the District's reasoned appeals, the Texas legislature in 1971 passed a law to license athletic trainers. Education qualifications were established for applicants, who were required to take and pass examinations administered by the Texas Board of Athletic Trainers.

Almost six years would elapse before the second state, Georgia, enacted licensure.

At the 1976 annual meeting, President Frank George announced formation of the Licensure Committee. Its assignment was to develop model licensure legislation and guidelines for imple-

1976 Board of Directors formed NATA's first Licensure Committee. Seated (L to R): Richard Malacrea, Robert White, Bill Flentje and Eddie Lane. Standing (L to R): Otho Davis (executive director), Craig Lewellyn, Warren Lee, Frank George (president), Bill Chambers, Tom Wall and John Anderson. Not shown: Wesley Jordan.

menting it. Eventually, the model bill was developed by the Committee and approved by the NATA Board.

Gradually, more states were added to the regulation column, which included licensure, the most clearly defined of the regulatory forms; others were certification and registration.

But it was a slipperier slope than anticipated. In some cases, the triumphs had to be regarded as only qualified successes. By 1988, with 18 states regulating athletic training, the movement slowed. For that, Ed Crowley, chair of the Licensure Committee, was thankful. He explained: "Actually, it's a positive reaction to what may have progressed to total chaos if we didn't slow down to evaluate what we have done thus far." Some current laws, he said, might be doing as much harm as good for athletic trainers.

At the heart of the problem was the transformation of the profession into multiple settings. Originally set up to regulate athletic training in the traditional high school-collegiate setting, the laws had become anachronisms.

"So, there was a need to grow with the profession, and legislatively, that creates a lot of headaches," declared Keith Webster, chair in 1998 of the Government Affairs Committee (formerly the Licensure Committee). "And when you try to either initiate new legislation or revise existing laws to reflect the changing scope of athletic training, that's when some are discouraged or disgusted with those laws."

NATA's support of licensing has been unswerving. Yet, the proximity with which it has been able to work with the state organizations—the groups that furnish the foot soldiers to work the legislatures—has depended on circumstances and interpretations of what's proper. In 1991, Dan Campbell, chair of the Government Affairs Committee at that time, announced the Association would not work actively with the state organizations to secure licensure. The prevailing view, he explained, was that it would be improper to use the dues of members in one state to support or oppose legislation in another state.

But things change. Since then, there has become available surplus money, a constitutional mechanism and measures of grass-roots accountability that have enabled the Association to collaborate with and support the state organizations in their initiatives.

As athletic training expands into new territory, it runs into other forms of health-care providers whose scope of practice—who and what they can treat—is not defined by the statutes. Therefore, the Association's goal has been and continues to be attaining legal standing for athletic trainers. Webster explained:

> We're still trying to pass legislation so that all 50 states have some form of regulation on the books. The concern is that without that, some may feel that what we practice may be called something else that is regulated, and thus we would be practicing illegally, violating someone else's practice act, whether it be medical or physical therapy or any other profession's legislation that's on the books. . . . We and the public need that type of recognition and protection.

Third-Party Reimbursement

When historians look for a single defining issue on America's political agenda of the 1990s—no easy task—much consideration will surely be given to medical care and how it is to be paid for. Expressed in terms of third-party reimbursement, it is certainly a big issue for athletic trainers.

Should athletic trainers be reimbursed for their services by a third-party payer? In a fax poll of NATA members in 1993, almost 93 percent said yes. It was a lopsided win for the argument that third-party reimbursement could supplement sports medicine budgets, allow athletic trainers to do more for athletes, and would give the profession greater status. On the other hand, opponents predicted turf wars with the physical therapists, increased insurance rates and the possibility that the profit motive would degrade the level of care.

"No other three words have caused as much concern, elation, ambivalence and discussion in the recent history of athletic training" as third-party reimbursement, Joe Godek wrote in *NATA News* in July 1995. Athletic trainers in sports medicine clinics saw third-party as their salvation, but athletic trainers in the traditional setting viewed it as the downfall of the profession, he declared.

Divisive as the issue was, it had the potential to be a unifying force, Godek believed. Third-party reimbursement was critical for athletic trainers in sports medicine clinics. But those in traditional settings also faced losing jobs as colleges and high schools were tempted to contract with for-profit corporations to reduce athletic training expenses.

The problem had first surfaced in the late 1980s, Dan Campbell wrote in *NATA News*. Even then some athletic trainers in the clinical setting were finding their employment tenuous. Employers saw them as financial liabilities because they were not revenue generators by nature. Campbell, chair of the Government Affairs Committee, elaborated:

> Added to that scenario were anecdotal instances where third-party payers were refusing reimbursement of fees for in-house physical therapy if any athletic trainer signed the clinical notes. These instances occurred even if the supervising physical therapist co-signed the note. It became apparent that if athletic trainers were to survive in the private sector, reimbursement of athletic training services by third-party payers would be necessary.

By early 1995, the NATA Board had appointed a Reimbursement Advisory Group. It was charged with developing and implementing a nationwide "outcomes" study, preparing a model approach to third-party payers (insurance companies and managed care organizations) and educating athletic trainers and related parties about reimbursement issues.

NATA leaders believed that insurance companies would not regard athletic trainers as legitimate reimbursable health-care providers without seeing evidence of the value of the care they provided. Obtaining this evidence was the purpose of the outcomes research.

BIO*Analyses Systems was contracted in 1996 to develop and implement the Athletic Training

Outcomes Assessment. To provide a comprehensive definition of outcomes, participating athletic trainers and patient/clients would rate the treatments and rehabilitation.

The first phase of the three-year study was completed in 1997. On a 0-to-4 scale, with 4 being tops, 2,408 patients rated their overall pre-treatment at 2.48. This rose dramatically to 3.55 after treatment by an athletic trainer. Of the most frequently used modalities, the most effective appeared to be cold packs, ice massages, heat packs, therapeutic exercise, functional activity exercises, electrotherapy and taping and bracing.

Completion of the outcomes study produced a finding of a high level of effectiveness and patient satisfaction with athletic training services. Pretty much what athletic trainers already knew, but now they had it in writing.

Marjorie Albohm, who chaired the Reimbursement Advisory Group, saw the issue of reimbursement as one of identity for the profession as much as it was to secure payment for athletic training services. She declared:

> It's not that we are just treating athletes anymore; it's being recognized as the health-care provider of choice for the physically active. That's what our efforts in reimbursement are really all about, and that's why it's so important to our profession. To grow in the future, we have to have that recognition. We have to be known as the health-care provider of choice for the physically active.

The morning line on attaining third-party reimbursement shows a formidable track. "I think it is not going to be something that will be resolved in the immediate future," President Kent Falb asserted in 1998. "We will continue to work at it, diplomatically and wisely . . . and when there are opportunities for us, we'll be ready to take advantage of them. But it is not going to be an easy process."

Job Satisfaction and Burnout

Athletic trainers—a community of happy campers?

All things considered, most of them think of their work in a positive vein. They tend to be a close-knit group of men and women, proud of what they do, enthusiastic about their work and enjoying those they work with. So why, then, have some athletic trainers quit the profession?

Job satisfaction among members has been an ongoing concern for the Association. It is probably the overarching reason for maintaining a professional organization. Focus on and secure job contentment and just about everything else falls in place.

When college athletic trainers were surveyed by the College/University Athletic Trainers' Committee in 1996, the report provided an earful. The athletic trainers complained that their job responsibilities were varied and sometimes didn't coincide with job descriptions. They also complained that their pay scales didn't compare with those of registered nurses or physician assistants. And more than 60 percent of the respondents reported work overload.

By its very nature, athletic training is a vocation inherent with conflict. The athletic trainer's No. 1 responsibility—protecting the athlete—can be at odds with the coaches' wish to keep their players in the lineup.

This problem has been expressed early and often. It was noted in a 1963 *Journal of the American Medical Association* report on a survey of AMA's Committee on the Medical Aspects of Sports. Praising NATA for "raising the calling of athletic training to a true profession," the report pointed to problems faced by all athletic trainers who were responsible to the coaches or who were hired by them. "The trainer," stated the report, "is in a position where he can be subjected to tremendous pressure by the coach concerning when athletes are physically fit for competition."

That was then. And now? Frank George observed in 1998:

Now I believe, and maybe it's only because I'm older and more solid in my position—I've been here 34 years—now I can't imagine a coach putting pressure on me to play someone who's injured or not ready to play. I'm thinking that that's the way it is everywhere, but it might not be

so. Young people, people who don't have control of their jobs, I'm sure they are having as many problems as we did in the old days.

By the mid-80s, the pressures on athletic trainers had become a frequent topic of research. Burnout, described by one researcher as a "syndrome of inappropriate attitudes towards clients and towards self," is associated with exhaustion, insomnia, migraines, ulcers and other emotional and physical conditions originating from the workplace.

A 1985 *Journal* article by Daniel Campbell; Michael H. Miller, Ph.D.; and Walter W. Robinson, Ph.D. described findings of a survey of athletic trainers. The report concluded that approximately 40 percent were "burned out and some are extremely burned out." Athletic trainers, the report further stated, "have a large assortment of medical conditions which appear to be more prevalent than would be expected in a population of relatively young men and women."

A year later, the *Journal* reported another study, this one by Susan A. Capel, Ph.D. Using a Maslach Burnout Inventory as methodology to study a sample of 332 athletic trainers, she concluded: "Burnout does exist among athletic trainers, although in the sample the burnout scores were only average."

Unfortunately, burnout and attainment of job satisfaction defy easy resolution. And in former President Mark Smaha's view, NATA's potential for solving the problem is limited.

He opined:

NATA is not a union. NATA can provide seminars and strategies on how to deal with burnout and long hours, etc. that can be helpful. But I don't think the NATA can be solely responsible for going to an employer and saying, "Gee, you need to do this because this guy's getting burnt out." They [NATA] can establish recommended standards for health care so far as the number of athletic trainers per athlete . . . but a lot of it is the responsibility of the athletic trainer. We can't put that burden solely on our organization.

8

THE GENDER NEUTRAL TRAINING ROOM

The Blossoms of Title IX

Most viewers were still watching their TV in black and white when Linda Treadway appeared as mystery guest on the popular CBS show called *What's My Line?* Panelists Dorothy Kilgallen, Arlene Francis and Bennett Cerf quizzed her for clues about her line of work. They were stumped, and not surprisingly. How could a woman possibly be an athletic trainer?

The training room had always been the sanctum of men and boys. The beginning of the end for that segregated preserve came when President Nixon signed into law the Higher Education Act of 1972. Title IX of that law prohibited sex discrimination in school and college athletic programs. That landmark piece of legislation was the Erie Canal that opened a vast migration of women into competitive sports. Accompanying them were women who were preparing themselves to treat their injuries.

There had been women athletic trainers prior to Title IX. The first female member of NATA, Dotty Cohen, had joined in early 1966 as an Indiana University graduate student. She was followed that same year by Sherry Kosek Babagian.

The gender change in the Association's constituency was duly noted in the *Journal*. Beginning in 1973, that publication had a new columnist, Holly Wilson, athletic trainer at Indiana State University.

Calling her column "Not for Men Only," she introduced it with an essay on the changing culture:

> The entry of women into the field of athletic training is a long overdue necessity, for we, too, have a moral obligation to our sports programs. Although presently there are few jobs available for women trainers, the need definitely exists, and it will certainly be a growing field as it becomes increasingly accepted and understood by women physical educators. The great rise in women's competition will certainly warrant the need for trained professional athletic trainers to properly care for the athletes.

Babagian, the second NATA female member, had another distinction. In 1972, she became the first woman to take the certification exam. It was a memorable experience. Since there were no coed training rooms at the time, she took the taping test in the hallway in the presence of a number of uninvited male onlookers. Nervous? Sure. "It was not ideal," she recalled, "but it was the way it was, and I got through it."

How was *the way it was?* For most of the early women, it could be intimidating. Because of their scant numbers, they were somewhat of a novelty. Such uniqueness tends to produce a sense of isolation. Marjorie Albohm recalls early meetings:

> I can remember one of the first meetings I attended 25 years ago in Kansas City and the

Karen Toburen (C) discusses issues with District 4 Director Denny Miller (L) and Director-Elect John Schrader (R).

awestruck feeling I had being there in this wonderful group of people, but no women. No spouses, no children. The men were very dedicated to being there and attending their meetings, and it was a strange feeling, but one that was just part of those times.

As they might have anticipated, women athletic trainers in the vanguard encountered some roadblocks. One was a physical, brick-and-mortar impediment. Until the 1970s, the gymnasiums and field houses had been built mostly for men. Integrating the existing locker rooms, showers and training rooms while preserving privacy required some ingenuity and a willingness on the part of both sexes to improvise.

There was also the challenge of altering mindsets. Karen Toburen, head of sports medicine athletic training programs at Southwest Missouri State, remembered the early resistance:

> When I needed the support, I often got it from the [male] athletic trainers. I found greater resistance from athletic directors and different levels of administration in terms of getting position descriptions and having them realize that female athletes also can get injured and how do we provide for that population?

The tests of mettle experienced by the early female athletic trainers were compellingly portrayed in Marcia Anderson's 1975 study, "Pioneer Women Athletic Trainers: Their Side of the Story." Chronicling the experiences of 13 women who practiced in the male-dominated profession during the 1960s and 70s, Anderson found in their accounts a number of hurdles that had to be surmounted.

One was in getting a foot in the door, and that involved obtaining education and experience. Initially, few schools offering programs in athletic training admitted women. Sometimes women were barred from the necessary classes because they were held in training rooms that were in the off-limits men's locker rooms. And in the days when women athletic trainers treated only women athletes, they did not have the benefit of best-quality training that comes with exposure to the collision sports like football.

Another component of quality preparation that the early women missed was supervision. Most of her interviewees, Anderson wrote, "strongly believe that lack of supervision afforded them by a qualified athletic trainer did more to limit their professional development than any other issue. This supervision could have provided them key clinical exposure to hands-on experience that was provided to their male counterparts, but limited or denied to women."

A hardship for early women athletic trainers, the demands of travel are still a cause of stress. Men experience it, too, but most athletic training staffs have more men to split up the away-game assignments.

There was room for women athletic trainers. "But not just any woman would do," wrote Linda Treadway in a 1974 issue of the *Journal*. She had covered the U.S. Women's Track and Field Trials in the 1972 Olympics and was surprised to find women athletic trainers for the events in short supply. "It [the profession] requires someone who believes in the value of athletics, can communicate and work with people, is willing to put in some long, hard hours, is level headed, and is not easily upset. The hours may be long, but the rewards are many."

Despite the obstacles and deprivation, one important element—the availability of a mentor—seemed to be there for most of the women. Katie Grove, chair of Women in Athletic Training Committee that NATA formed in 1996, said the women she worked with "all had at least one very

good male mentor who has been very supportive, and has really gotten them going . . . I think they would all say that there was somebody along the way that didn't look at gender, and that encouraged them and pushed them."

Once established in the profession, women found some of their problems to be not so different from men. Women comprised about a third of NATA's certified membership in 1989 when John LeGear, editor of *NATA News* at the time, wrote an article headlined "Women Aim To Improve ATC's Quality of Life." Consensus of the women interviewed was that their frustrations— long hours, insufficient pay, too many bosses— were also experienced by the opposite sex. But they also had to contend with an issue that wasn't so high on the male agenda—the time demands of raising children.

Gaining in Numbers and Influence

NATA's Board first took formal notice of women in the profession in 1974 when it established the Ad Hoc Committee on Women. Chaired by Holly Wilson, the Committee was to identify the needs

Tennis star Gabriella Sabatini (L) made a guest appearance on behalf of the Women in Athletic Training Committee (WATC) at NATA's 49th Annual Meeting & Clinical Symposia in Baltimore, MD. WATC Committee Member Kathleen Stroia (C) arranged Sabatini's appearance.

GAIL A. WELDON

Her life was short, but Gail Weldon made the most of the time she had.

When she joined NATA in the early 1970s, she was one of the first women in the membership. There would be more, a lot more, of her gender that would follow, and she applied herself to women's issues, serving on the Ad Hoc Committee on Women from 1972–74.

She had other interests, too. In 1976, she was selected for the U.S. Olympic team medical staff, another first for women in athletic training. She served as an athletic trainer for several Olympic games, and from 1989 to 1991, she was a director of the U.S. Olympic Festival.

Children's health and fitness was another Weldon concern. She founded KIDFIT in 1989 as a nonprofit organization to improve the fitness level of the nation's youth. By the time of her untimely death at age 40 in 1991, KIDFIT had received state and national recognition.

Her pioneer work on behalf of women athletic trainers was recognized in 1995 when she became the first woman to be inducted in the Hall of Fame.

of women athletic trainers and recommend ways that NATA could help them advance in the profession.

Some women complained that they were being left out, denied positions of leadership in NATA. No, said others, the problem was that many women were content to sit on the sidelines and not get involved. Operator of a women's fitness clinic in Los Angeles, Gail Weldon gave her view in a 1989 issue of *NATA News*:

> It's all very well that more women are coming in, but the important thing is that they participate in governing the NATA, work with NATA committees and assist on special projects. It isn't enough to stand on the outside complaining about the lack of fairness or inequality. Women must work together with men to make athletic training better for everyone.

By the mid-1980s, women were assuming more visible roles of responsibility in NATA affairs. About that time, Janice Daniels had been elected to the Board, the first female director. In 1991, Julie Max became vice president of the Board. And at the end of the Association's first half century, women were heading such important institutions as the NATABOC and the Research and Education Foundation.

The progress of women in athletic training could be measured in statistics. In 1996, they constituted 44 percent of NATA's membership. They also held 26 percent of the Board, committee and liaison positions. More impressive than the statistics, however, was the alacrity with which the numbers were changing.

The women are looking to NATA to keep the door open to them for leadership positions. Grove stated:

> I think we tend to pick and stay with people who are similar to us. So when it comes time for picking committees and those kinds of things, if you're a male, you tend to think of a male. People need to remember that there are other people out there. One of the ways this is being accomplished is by the development of female state representatives who report to members of the Women in Athletic Training Committee.

To the credit of the Association and the profession, leadership opportunities for women had become almost a non-issue by century's end. In 1999, Peggy Houglum, chair of the Education Council's Continuing Education Committee, observed:

> I can say right now that the Board of Directors is very sensitive to women's issues. If you take a look

at the Board today—there are actually three women sitting on that Board of Directors. That's historical. I think that's a significant thing. I think there are more women on committees now who are going to have an impact not only on the decisions that are made within the committees but also the attitudes of the committees towards women.

Parity within Reach?

The goal of women athletic trainers—parity with men—seemed close at the end of NATA's first half century. But it wasn't quite there yet.

The athletic training rooms of professional sports team, for example, were still almost as much all-male fraternities as they had been 50 years earlier. "For the most part," stated Toburen, "the NFL and NBA are closed to us. In terms of truly having all doors open to us, they're not there. There can be male trainers for any of the female offerings that we have in the United States, but it doesn't go the opposite way. It isn't equal for women."

Not that all women athletic trainers are hell-bent on working the pros. "My guess," conjectured Houglum, "is that they realize that pro sports is not an easy life, and it requires a lot of travel and a lot of time away from home and family and friends. For that whole season, it interferes socially, and they may not be willing to make that sacrifice."

Obviously, there is no legislated equalizer that provides a foolproof formula for doing it all—working long hours, dedicating time to the profession, and then raising the family.

This "family life issue" certainly is not confined to athletic training. Like so many things, it is a reflection of society in general. But as NATA's second half-century approached, Grove was hopeful:

> I think that the Association as a whole is now used to seeing families with kids, and I think that certainly is a positive change. There are a lot of little things. For example, we happen to hear a lot more men say, "I can't be there for that meeting, because my daughter has a game." These types of things were uncommon 20 years ago.

Undeniably, nearly 30 years of Title IX have brought an incandescent change to athletic

---

JANICE DANIELS

When Janice Daniels was elected to the NATA Board in 1984 as the first woman director, she wasn't sure what to expect. "I remember hearing some stories from the previous district director," she recalled. "I think he thought it was going to be tough."

Actually, being the trailblazer turned out to be a piece of cake.

"I remember Otho Davis at the first meeting," she said. "He came out and he was like, just take your time, relax, and he was being very nice to me. . . . My overwhelming feeling was that I was very well accepted. I tremendously enjoyed the men I was working with."

Not that Board service didn't have its challenges. For Daniels and her colleagues, the real test was in getting prepped for Board meetings which, at that time, were longer than today's streamlined sessions. She said, "It was just being up on all the material. Being a full-time worker and yet being well prepared for the meetings was probably the biggest challenge."

All the preparation was necessary, too, because the Board during Daniels' six-year tenure had a lot on its plate. It was in the process of successfully orchestrating the acquisition of the international headquarters in Dallas and the transition from a volunteer to a paid, full-time staff.

training. And while women have been the main beneficiaries, men, too, in allocation of resources, sharing of workloads and in other ways, could be warmed by the radiation.

JULIE MAX

Vice president of the NATA Board is an appointed position, and in 1991, Julie Max was the choice of her Board colleagues, the first woman to hold that post. Not surprisingly, she remembered her experience working with an otherwise male Board to be congenial.

She declared, "I never encountered one negative due to my gender. . . . I was never given any indication that I was not accepted or that I should not be there."

Subbing for the Association president when that person was unavailable, Max found her challenges to be the same as the other directors: address the issues and make the best decisions possible.

Certified in 1979, Max spent the next 20 years working at California State-Fullerton, a school, she said, that fosters a philosophy akin to her own: never forget your roots. She stated, "I think it's very important that our young people never forget the people that were instrumental in creating roots for them. . . . We all need to be reminded of why we are where we are and who got us there."

For Max and her gender contemporaries, the roots go back to women she calls the "foremothers" of athletic training. Does she admire them? "Absolutely. No question," she said. "We would not be where we are today if they hadn't persevered."

9

ENRICHING WITH ETHNIC DIVERSITY

Underrepresentation: Symphony without the Woodwinds and Brass

The influx of women into the profession was not matched by racial and ethnic minorities. This was a surprise to many. By the time Wilt Chamberlain and Oscar Robertson were dominating NCAA basketball in the mid-1950s, blacks and other nonwhites had established a growing presence on both collegiate and professional teams. But among those who administered the athletic training rooms, where were the African-Americans, the Hispanics, the Asiatics?

Jack Rockwell pondered this question in print. In the winter 1968 issue of the *Journal*, he remarked:

> With newspaper and magazine articles telling of requests for black coaches and black trainers at various places across the country, we find ourselves faced with two questions. The first is, Why aren't there more black athletic trainers now working in all phases of athletics today? It is not because of any single or significant reasons, but it must be remedied.
>
> The second question that arises then is why should an athletic trainer be differentiated by skin color? This is where understanding is needed; the black athlete should not, cannot, and must not be treated in any way differently from the white athlete. . . . As individual athletic trainers who all have pride in your work, and display the integrity

and character needed to perform your tasks, I sincerely hope you will all show the greatest concern and understanding in this situation that prevails in our country today.

Twenty years later, the same questions were being asked. The training rooms were still largely staffed by whites. Of the nearly 14,800 certified athletic trainers in 1998, there were only 138 blacks, 271 Hispanics, 64 American Indians, 204 classified as Asian-Pacific Islander, and a little more than a thousand who were not identified by ethnicity.

What these statistics reflected was the fact that, at least in the case of blacks, there actually had been a shrinkage. In the early days, there had been large numbers of African-Americans performing as athletic trainers.

"Clubhouse men" is what they were often called, according to Frank Walters. The first person to chair NATA's Ethnic Minority Advisory Group, Walters recounted: "They were the guys who did everything, just like the old athletic trainers did. They gave rubdowns, massages, they cleaned up, picked up, did the laundry, took care of the clubhouse itself. There wasn't much of anything they didn't do."

John Harvey, Texas Southern University, witnessed the work of the early black athletic trainers. He had tagged along with his

NASEBY RHINEHART

He may not have been the first African American athletic trainer, but Naseby Rhinehart was certainly among the trail-blazers. He began his career in the training room of the University of Montana in 1935, a month after being graduated from that school. As an undergraduate athlete, he won nine letters in football, basketball and track.

Like most other athletic trainers of that day, Rhinehart did not have the benefit of either curriculum or apprenticeship. He learned his craft mostly by doing. But what he learned would be passed on to almost two generations of student athletic trainers that interned under his supervision.

HENRY "BUDDY" TAYLOR

Citing the likes of a strand of Olympic superstars like Wilma Rudolph and Ralph Boston, Buddy Taylor once announced, "I have trained more Olympic gold medal winners than any other athletic trainer in the country."

That's quite a claim. But, then, Buddy Taylor had quite a career.

Not yet in college, Taylor got his start in 1948 as an athletic trainer with the Richmond (VA) Colts baseball team. When he was graduated from Indiana University, he was the first African American to earn a master's degree in athletic training.

As an athletic trainer for the Maccabeah Games in Tel Aviv in 1969, he met Max Novich, a sports medicine physician. Together they would subsequently author a text, *Training and Conditioning of Athletes*. Taylor's expertise in treating low back pain and hamstring injuries would lead to publication in the *Journal* and presentation at NATA's 1969 annual meeting.

Taylor served as athletic trainer for the Utah Stars in the American Basketball Association and augmented his long list of "firsts" by becoming the first black president of a professional team athletic training association, namely the organization for the ABA.

In 1974, he went back to the campus as assistant professor and head athletic trainer at Winston-Salem State University.

A description Taylor once wrote of his role as athletic trainer was certainly definitive of the profession. "To the players," he said, "I am a combination medicine man, close friend, confidant, psychologist and father confessor. To both the coach and the team physician, I am an advisor and an aide."

grandfather and the athletic trainer of the old Houston Buffaloes to the team's Texas League games. These men, he said, were basically servants. "That's why, today, one of the biggest emphases in athletic training is that you serve, you serve the athlete. That's where the service attitude developed," he stated.

Then came the formation of NATA. Ironically, the new Association's emphasis on education, so instrumental in developing the profession, also led to the near extinction of the early black athletic trainers. Harvey declared:

> When the athletic trainers in the university setting decided to establish a profession out of this thing and they wanted a college degree, well, all of those people were lost. Very few of those locker room people had the qualifications, with the exception of Naseby [Rhinehart] and people like that. Those people who had credentials were in place, but those that didn't have them were kind of pushed aside.

Although published research on blacks and other ethnic minorities in athletic training is sparse, portions of a noteworthy study on certification and employment appeared in NATA's 1998 annual meeting "Proceedings." The authors, Frank Walters, Ph.D., and Eric Howard, EdD, contended that many early black athletic trainers, isolated from the necessary information and those who could supervise them, could not take advantage of the "grandfather" route to certification and, therefore, never became credentialed.

Nevertheless, there were a number of African-American athletic trainers from the early days who persevered and went on to become influential beyond their race. In 1935, Naseby Rhinehart began his long career at the University of Montana. Chester Grant, a fixture at North Carolina State for 30 years, had been highly

Marsha Grant Ford, the first African-American woman to become certified, works with an athlete.

respected by players and coaches. Dr. Charles W. Turner, a licensed chiropractor as well as an athletic trainer, had an illustrious career that included treating U.S. Olympic teams beginning in 1928. And certainly the profession would have been poorer had it not been for the contributions of Henry (Buddy) Taylor, the "clubhouse man" of the old Richmond Colts baseball team who went on to co-author the highly acclaimed text, *Training and Conditioning of Athletes.*

As gender issues began to surface, ethnic minority women entering the profession encountered challenges similar to their white counterparts; some claim even more so because of race. Shortly after Marcia Anderson completed her study of early women athletic trainers, Marsha Grant Ford did similar research for a paper entitled "Pioneer Ethnic Minority Women." Most of the women had reported experiencing discrimination of some form.

Years later, Grant Ford, the first African-American woman to become certified, said she would encourage ethnic minority women interested in athletic training to become as prepared as they can. "The things that your mother told you about how you had to be 200 percent better, that's all true," she declared.

But she would also remind these potential recruits that there "are men and women out there that are interested in you as a professional. And they will take an interest in you. I don't want them [prospective athletic trainers] to think the whole world is so callous and there's no one out there who is going to help them. Because that hasn't been my experience."

Experiences of Other Ethnic Populations

Other ethnic minorities also share the early history in athletic training. Among those registered for the meeting that gave birth to NATA in 1950 were Lincoln Kimura, San Jose State University, and Frank Medina, University of Texas.

FRANK E. MEDINA

A part Cherokee Indian, Medina was for many years head athletic trainer at the University of Texas. Representing District 6, he served on the first NATA Board of Directors in 1950.

In addition to being twice named "Trainer of the Year" by the Rockne Club Foundation, he served on the Texas Governor's Commission on Physical Fitness and as a consultant in 1964 to the President's Council on Physical Fitness.

During his career, he accumulated a number of awards and honors, and shortly after his retirement, he was inducted into the Helms Hall of Fame in 1965.

The experience among non-black minorities in athletic training appears to have been pretty much mainstream.

Hazel Ando, a third generation Japanese and one of the subjects of Grant Ford's study, said, "I don't feel I hit any obstacles at all by being an Asian. It was more of a gender issue—being a female." She added, "I never heard anyone say, Because I'm Asian, I didn't get the job."

Ando, who in 1999 was president of the California Athletic Trainers Association, felt NATA has been supportive of Asian Americans in the profession. She saw the influx of international members from Japan and South Korea as contributing to a comparatively easy assimilation into the athletic training culture.

For Hispanics, perhaps the biggest barrier in athletic training has been the language. And it has been an obstacle confined primarily to first-generation Hispanic-Americans, observed Ben Carbajal, who had served on the Advisory Council. Since the first generation's offspring tended to be bilingual, they have found it much easier to gain entry and be assimilated into the profession. Skiffs and conduct, rather than ethnicity, seems to be the determiner. Explained Carbajal:

This is a people profession and you have to conduct yourself in a responsible, professional manner and, hopefully, people will see that and allow your actions to speak for yourself. There

may be situations—and I'm sure there are—where that may not be enough. But I try not to focus on that . . . I don't hear people making a big issue of [perceived discrimination] among Hispanic trainers.

The NATA Response

The dearth of ethnic minorities in athletic training has not been ignored by NATA leadership. As a body, they genuinely seemed to recognize that the music sounds better when the orchestra is complete. To understand the needs of minority athletic trainers and to attract more of them to the profession, the Board in the mid-1980s created the Minority Athletic Trainers Committee. Although it went on to establish a pair of scholarships for minority athletic trainers and published some brochures, the Committee languished because of insufficient direction. It was disbanded in 1991.

Dissolving the Committee was the Board's way of recognizing that more needed to be done. The dismissal was accompanied that year by the formation of the Ethnic Minority Advisory Council. The role of the Advisory Council was to identify professional concerns of minority and ethnic athletic trainers and bring them to the Board's attention. Frank Walters, who was appointed to head the Advisory Council, was hopeful. "In the black community, students are often athletes. If they become familiar with our profession, they may look at athletic training as a career opportunity," he speculated.

René Revis Shingles, who subsequently became chair of the Advisory Council, agreed that attaining visibility was essential. She said:

> When you look at African-Americans in particular, African-Americans are predominately in and around the urban centers in the U.S. or in the South. And many of those urban or rural schools do not have athletic trainers. Therefore, students are not aware of athletic training as a profession. They do not have a role model.
>
> . . . As part of our public relations efforts, I think we have to get into some of the ethnic publications that the lay people have access to. [We have] to make sure these publications get to the high schools, to the counselors, [we have to] go to career days.

When the Advisory Council was formed, it set out to pursue five goals. In addition to those designed to attract more ethnic minorities to the profession and facilitate their educational preparation, the group sought to introduce ethnic minority topics to NATA-sponsored educational programs and symposia. Reflecting on the progress being made, Walters reported success in a venue at the annual meetings. Topics relevant to ethnic minorities were being presented. But the health-related subjects were also pertinent to non-minority athletic trainers who, he lamented, were ignoring these presentations.

The behavior and attitudes of some individuals may be faulted, but those who would do so understand that the profession tends to mirror general society. Few, however, see NATA policy and process as anything other than hospitable and supportive of minorities.

"I can say this: I know that when I was chairperson of the Ethnic Minority Advisory Council, there wasn't anything that we put forward that was ever denied [by the Board]," Walters declared. "And I don't think that was an attempt just to placate us."

When Ronnie Barnes arrived in the late 1960s, what he got was a lot of encouragement that inspired him to become involved. And he did, along the way becoming chair of the Research and Education Foundation. He observed:

> . . . I think that the biggest concern of minorities within the Association was that there were just so few of them. And so, what we wanted NATA to do was to begin a recruitment program to look at some predominantly black neighborhoods and get information out. . . . And the NATA has done an excellent job with that. It's an ongoing process. It's evolutionary. But I think that the NATA can get an excellent grade on its report card with respect to minority issues.

10

FROM HERE TO HEREAFTER

Not Your Father's Oldsmobile

In an attempt to appeal to younger car buyers, a Detroit advertising agency sought to convince them that the client's automobile was no longer the conservative model—by their standards anyway—that their parents had driven. The ad campaign didn't sell as many cars as had been expected and was dropped the following year. The slogan, however, caught attention as a motto for dramatic change.

After 50 years, athletic trainers have a profession that is not their father's model, either. The fact that the profession has changed so dramatically is not particularly remarkable. So has everything else. What is notable, however, is that it has undergone a great continental drift. As Chad Starkey, chair of the Education Council, observed, athletic training started out in one profession (athletics) and wound up in another (health care).

Some advances are seen in the culture itself. For example, where are all those tight-lipped originals, the ones who played everything close to their vests? Six years after NATA's founding, Bill Linskey, Public Relations Committee chair, was noticing—exultantly—their disappearance. Referring to the taping panel at the 1956 annual meeting, he wrote in the *Journal*:

> It is a treat to see trainers demonstrate their various techniques for the benefit of others. What

a difference between 1956 and 1926. Now everyone is willing to show how he does it, and no one has anything to conceal. Share and share alike for the benefit of the injured athlete these days.

In stark contrast with the early provincialism and closeting of trade secrets, the Association and the profession have become ecumenical, networking with other athletic trainers throughout the world. The membership rolls have come to include individuals from Japan, Korea, Great Britain, Spain and other nations. This prompted the Board to create a task force to pursue an international agenda. At the 1998 annual meeting in Baltimore, the World Federation of Athletic Trainers Task Force hosted a World Congress. The objective was to find out what was being done worldwide for the physically active and which countries were interested and involved in athletic training. Forty participants from 11 countries participated. If there is any such thing as a sure bet, it is that early in the 21st century, NATA and the profession will have expanded to a new frontier, and it will be global.

NATA has periodically and informally probed the waters of change, providing a time line of progress. In 1972, a *Journal* article published responses to the question, What is the greatest change in athletic training? For Ken Rawlinson, NATA's third Board chair, it was recognition of the value and use of water, salts and fluids during practices and games. Five physicians in sports medicine answered: "status of program, educational levels, methods of care and prevention of heat stress illness."

Twenty-one years later, *NATA News* was reporting the biggest changes noticed by three veteran athletic trainers: Larry Gardner, Mark Smaha and Steve Tollefson. They listed:

1. Increased level of professionalism.

2. Use of computers in treatment, allowing for more in-depth analysis.

3. Advancement in surgical techniques that permit more aggressive treatment.

4. OSHA standards that regulate treatment of bloody injuries so as to minimize the risk of HIV and hepatitis B.

5. Numerical growth of the profession, leading many to gravitate to physical therapy and industrial settings.

The same question, asked of NATA leaders, was answered in a 1998 *NATA News* article, "Progress of the Profession: Athletic Training Matures, Sets Stage for Future":

• Diverse practice settings, challenge to redefine role and establish position in health care (Marjorie Albohm)

• Growth (Eve Becker-Doyle)

• Certification procedure, being recognized by the American Medical Association as an allied health-care profession (Kent Falb)

• Diversity of practice setting (Denise Fandel)

• Movement from athletic profession to health-care profession (Chad Starkey)

Aside from these snippets of perceived changes, the half-century of progress in athletic training can be compressed into a four-screen diorama:

Treatment

"Sports medicine has changed so much in the last 30 years. It's been just incredible," Frank George declared in retrospect:

Twenty-five, thirty years ago, a guy [would have] an ACL [anterior cruciate ligament] injury, and they didn't know what to do for it. . . . There was no surgery to repair it in those days . . . The advent of the arthoscope has changed so much in sports medicine in its surgical procedures. But we would do tests in the training room; our team doctors would do tests, and we'd say, maybe it's this . . . One look at the arthoscope would tell us how wrong we were. . . . The arthoscope has made us much better clinicians, and the MRI is doing the same thing.

Proliferation of Practice Settings

"Did we 50 years ago ever believe that we would be in the corporate, clinical and industrial settings?" The answer to Kent Falb's rhetorical question must almost certainly be no.

As the population of athletic trainers mushroomed, it surpassed the capacity of the traditional setting of colleges and secondary schools to absorb them. Providentially, employment opportunities were emerging elsewhere—in the clinics, offices and factories. Seventy percent of workmen's compensation claims were for sprains and strains. No surprise, then, when the profession collectively asserted: *Who better than us are equipped to treat them?*

Consequently, the term "physically active" became ensconced in the athletic trainer's vocabulary to encompass the broadened career market. The range of patients went from dancers to joggers to the company softball team. To athletic trainers, the only difference was that, unlike amateur and professional athletes, the physically active were not always physically fit.

So it came to be that by 1998, only 34 percent of athletic trainers were employed in the college and secondary schools. Of the rest, almost half could be found in non-traditional settings that included sports medicine clinics, fitness complexes, government agency training facilities and corporations.

Not that the migration to new kinds of workplaces pleased everyone. One dissenting athletic trainer protested in *NATA News:*

I entered the field of athletic training to treat athletes, not factory workers. When an athletic trainer concerns him- or herself with the overall profits of some company rather than the progress of his/her patient, then the integrity of our profession is lost.

Despite misgivings—and they are held by more than a few individuals—the profession seems likely to seek new practice settings rather than back away from non-traditional ones where beachheads have already been established. And some of the future work arenas might seem mind-blowing unimaginable to today's athletic trainers. Expansion, in Falb's view, is not a matter of choice:

As the athletic trainer expands into multiple-practice settings and those that are yet unforeseen, there are those who may think this is not good. But, to expand and to develop, the athletic training profession needs to continue to change. It needs to expand and go into these areas because we do have the membership, we do have the skills, we have the knowledge and we certainly can be a vital part of the health-care industry.

Professional Preparation

As in many things, there is a linkage: the ability of athletic trainers to enter non-traditional settings, as well as to treat college and secondary school athletes—a connection that never could have been made without rigorous preparation. Starting from scratch, the profession came to have more quality educational programs than Woodstock had rock bands and a means to test and certify athletic trainers' preparation, perpetuating self-development through continuing education. These accomplishments far surpassed Lindsy McLean's initial goal of developing education to save the profession from individuals whose only qualification was being buddies with the coaches.

Obviously, education is an endless activity, subject to periodical re-evaluation and revision. Education Reform is the instrument adopted by NATA to meet whatever the 21st century requires for practicing in diverse settings.

At the end of NATA's "first fifty," Education Reform had amassed widespread support, at least conceptually. On many of the specifics, there were some athletic trainers who had reservations.

Recognition and Acceptance

Central to all of NATA's efforts to upgrade the profession was securing legitimacy for athletic training. Becoming a member of the club. Being recognized as a bonafide player in the allied health-care lineup. Without that, all the accomplishments to better the profession would have been, to some degree, unfulfilling. And just as bad, absence of this recognition by peers would have impaired the profession in the marketplace.

But recognition was achieved in two forms: regulation of the practice by state legislatures and acceptance by other health-care providers, chief of which was the American Medical Association. Reflecting on that, Gary Delforge, who did so much to shape professional education, called AMA's endorsement "probably one of the most gratifying events that I personally was involved in. It left individuals, I think, unanimously across the country with the gratifying feeling that we have arrived, we have arrived!"

Voices of Experience

The Association's leaders who have been there, done that are a valuable resource. What would they say to those who will guide the profession as it seeks to emulate and surpass the progress of the last 50 years?

Mark Smaha, president 1988–92, on jobs and where they will come from: "Until we can find the right compromise between creating more jobs and making it more difficult to get into the profession, we're going to find a supply and demand problem." But beware, he declared, of attempting to cast athletic trainers in roles which they have no hope of playing successfully.

Otho Davis, executive director 1971–89, on licensing the practice in non-traditional settings: "Until you have the credential, don't break the

NATA's presidents from 1970 to 1999 (L to R): Kent Falb, Denny Miller, Mark Smaha, Jerry Rhea, Bobby Barton, William Chambers, Frank George and Bobby Gunn.

law. . . . And when the states say you can, then that's great, but until you get the state law, you've got a problem."

Lindsy McLean, architect of certification and NATABOC chair from 1970–79, on the right reasons for becoming an athletic trainer:

> . . . the profession started with the hands-on-caring, wanting-to-help-other-people attitude. As you get more and more involved in the academics, you cannot lose that, because you can educate people with an awful lot of practical and theoretical knowledge, but they've got to want to take care of people. . . . Because we're never going to be rich, it's getting better, but . . . you simply are not going to get the satisfaction in any way except for the satisfaction of helping other individuals."

McLean, again, on education: "We have to make sure we adapt [our education] to the job market. It's not certain where all our jobs are going to be 15 years from now. . . . As the health-care industry changes, we have to be on our guard against complacency and continuing to educate people the way we always have."

Frank George, president 1974–78, on sustaining camaraderie in the face of bigness:

> We can be up for the biggest game, the biggest rivalry and a lot of animosity between the two teams, the coaches, but guess what? The two trainers can be best friends and like each other and enjoy each other's company . . . I hope we don't lose that closeness, even though we're getting awfully big. There was a time when you could go to a national convention and you'd know everybody there. . . . The only thing the oldtimers lament is the loss of closeness, but I don't think there is. I think you [can go to a convention now] and know and see 95 or 100 people, have a good time with them, and there happens to be another 9,000 people that you don't know. We have to realize that that's okay.

Mark Smaha on sustaining cohesiveness in the face of bigness:

Large organizations tend to fragment. You have this and that group or committee. I think that weakens the strength of the organization. Sometimes I think that's a message for the organization—maybe you're not doing the job you need to be doing in addressing some of those issues, so we need to break away and do our own. Those things can happen to a large organization. . . . Sometimes we need to keep things simple. We need to find a mid-range, because if we try to intellectualize too much, we get headed off in a direction that I don't think is healthy.

Bobby Gunn, Board chairman and president 1968–1974, on disagreements: "I would beg them [future NATA leaders] to have open disagreements. You negate your problems when you bring them out in the open."

Kent Falb, president 1996–2000, on the athletic trainers' quality of life:

I think the leadership needs to continue to enhance the quality of life for our future colleagues. So they don't have to think they have to work 80 hours a week and they have to sacrifice their health and their families. They have done that long enough. They have to develop their self-esteem, and don't be hesitant, don't be intimidated into thinking that well, you're violating some unwritten code of ethics. We can still serve and still work with the same work ethic, but we don't have to prostitute ourselves any longer, because we have reached the position of an approved health-care provider. We don't have to prove ourselves. I think that equitable payment and work schedules and lifestyles should be something they should continue to strive for.

Eve Becker-Doyle, who has managed the Association since 1993 as executive director, on what volunteers mean to the future of NATA:

With Pinky Newell as a model, volunteers made this Association and the profession it represents. The members who gave so generously of their time and counsel—they were indispensable to NATA's success. Will volunteers be as important in the next 50 years? Absolutely! And because the members know it is *their* Association, I'm confident they will come forward.

So, What Happens on the Road to 2050?

Every era begins with some carryover from the preceding age. And from its first half century, the Association and the profession carry over an action file full of unfinished business. Pick an issue—third-party reimbursement, licensure, job satisfaction, multiple-practice settings—are any likely to be brought to a successful resolution within, say, the next generation?

A prognostication on third-party reimbursement from Frank George:

We are the original managed-care people. We have a lot of experience in it. We know what we're doing with it, and I think that's where the future of athletic training 15 years from now is going. I think insurance companies will realize, guess what? Athletic training is a good bargain. . . . Athletic trainers are generally very aggressive with their rehabilitation and getting the patients better. That's what is a little different from, I'll say, a hospital model. They [athletic trainers] see their patients a lot, they see them daily. I think that's what is going to keep athletic training afloat, keep it going, because it works.

But other imponderables may influence the importance of the victory. Mark Smaha on that subject:

Potentially, third-party reimbursement will be brought to resolution in favor of athletic trainers. However, by that time, health-care reform may have had a revolution, and that may be a moot point. I don't mean we should stop trying, because you don't have any forecast for that other issue.

And sometimes issues never leave. For Kent Falb, NATA's key objectives on entering the Second Fifty are Education Reform, third-party reimbursement, state regulatory acts, and recognition for athletic trainers as health-care providers. And they will have an interminable shelf life. He predicted:

I don't personally see any of those four objectives will ever come to conclusion, because a project or challenge is never completed. But what it does is to create newer, different and sometimes greater challenges. So prior programs and issues never really reach ultimate conclusion. They take on a new dimension.

As one coiner of neat maxims has observed, history is the science of what never happens twice. That is not altogether true. Many of the challenges of the next 50 years will turn out to be derivatives of the first half century. Which is not to say they can necessarily be treated with the same applications used in the past. But in building the house of NATA, the founders and their successors have left on deposit some constructive experience that can be helpful to future Association leaders as they concentrate on home improvement. The profession's forebears have also left some excellent guiding principles, particularly No. 4 of the Code of Ethics: *Members shall maintain high standards in the provision of service.* If future athletic trainers accept that precept as a command and not a suggestion, they will not only maintain the moral high ground but also avoid a lot of collisions with speed bumps on the road to the 2050 centennial.